I0570125

RE-VISION

A story of restoration, redemption, and the path to reach them both.

DANIEL DRUMWRIGHT

Copyright© 2024 Daniel Drumwright. All rights reserved.
No part of this publication may be reproduced, distributed,
or transmitted in any form or by any means, including
photocopying, recording, or other electronic or mechanical
methods, without the prior written permission of the
publisher, except in the case of brief quotations embodied in
critical reviews and certain other noncommercial uses
permitted by copyright law. For permission requests, inquire
to the publisher at the following website:
www.danieldrumwright.com

I thank God for the path that led me to this book. I never thought that I would say this, but the trials and tribulations I've faced have been the crucible in which these words were forged.

Daniel Drumwright

CONTENTS

Part Two

ACKNOWLEDGMENTS

This memoir wouldn't have come to be without the incredible support of many people. First, I'd like to thank my family and friends for their unwavering encouragement and patience throughout this journey. Specifically, I would like to thank my wife, Brandy, who has supported me throughout my health circumstances and the process of writing and releasing my memoir; My children, Blake, Bellami, and Beckham for being my biggest motivation; My aunt and uncle Marion and Decosta Jenkins Sr, who loved on me and provided a safe place for me to recover from my ordeal; My aunt and uncle, John and Freda Pinkerton , who spoke life into me and got me back and forth when I was able to get back to work: my aunt, Brenda Wynn, who has advocated for me and helped guide me through the publishing process; my aunts, Catina Clark, Lorita Covington, Diane Brown, Marina Jenkins, Sharon Parrish, Regina Newsome, Sigrid Coure,Tamina Jenkins, and NeNe Newsome; My uncles John Jenkins, Toney Covington Sr, Emmitt Wynn II, James Wynn, Styric McClure, James Harper Sr, Michael Buchanan, Russell Perkins, Jerry Shelton, Alex Coure, Ronnie Haywood, Joe Jenkins Jr, Joseph Jenkins, Anthony Jenkins, and John "Buck" Buchanan; my father and mother, Verlinda and Estle Drumwright, for the love and life you made for me and my siblings; my brothers, David and Darrell, who provided a safe place for me to ex-press myself and offered their help in so many ways; my cousins, Decosta Jenkins Jr, Toney Covington Jr, Mia Jenkins, Bryan Covington, Kiya Jordan, Jamela Jen-kins, Joe Lee, Ryan Lee, Davien Wynn, Emmett Wynn III, Victor Wynn, Latanya Newsome, Jermont Newsome, Lizz Jenkins, Damien Wynn Sr, Damien Wynn Jr, Erin Booker, Brian Ward, Keisha Micheaux, and Alecia Wynn; to my Friends and Dunnies, Tracy Carter, Nick Hodge, JW Murphy, Theo Townsend, King Dunlap, Devon Hackett, Jermaine Shute, Vincent Bradford, Devin Arnold, Taylor Brad-ford, Antione Caldwell, Brandon Blackman, Alex Mitthivong, Walter Morgan, Rolando Shannon, Sly Lee, Jadon Hogan, Deon Weeden, Tremayne Townsend, Jeremy Dupree, Josh Bone, Reggie Pope, Curtis Ewing, Corey Adkisson, Joe Towner, Brian Baker, Bryan Torrain, Jesse Green, Reggie McLaurine, Chase Bruce, Quinton Eskridge , Devin Arnold, Brandon Blackman, David Miller, Ashley Rob-inson, Steve Adkerson, Rachel Suell, Carolyn Adkerson, Ashleigh Moses, Jessica Barkley, and Natalie Fletcher; my mother-in-law, Rhonda Braden; my sister-in-law Latanya Drumwright; to my nephews, Demarkus and Demarius Drumwright ; to my other in-laws Jovan Hines, Erica Fuqua, Tanya Fuqua, Yolanda Phillips, Tony Williams IV, Valencia Phillips, Jennifer Simpson-Gooch, Bianca Fuqua, Brian Coure, Eric Coure, Eryn Coure, Courtney Hines, Johnathan Buchanan, Jermaine Hines, Gianna Flemings, Regina Garth, Ty Garth, Rasheeda Garth,

Pastor & Sister Murray and Family, the rest of my extended family; to my doctors Eric Schneider, Nancy Wolfe-Sidberry, James Sudberry, Jack Erter, Jim Sweeney, Candace Murphy-Reddick, Michael Pulitzer, Erich Gross, and Nataly Bailey: to my friends and former co-workers at the Tennessee Education Lottery, Former Mayor Karl Dean and staff, Judge Sheila Calloway and the Davidson County Juvenile Justice Center staff, Michelle Hernandez-Lane, Talia O'dneal-Lomax, Dennis Rowland and the Department of Finance for the Metropolitan Government Nashville and Davidson County. Their belief in me fueled my motivation, even during some of my most challenging moments.

I'm so grateful to my church community, The Temple Church, for providing a space of love and inspiration. Their support helped to foster the spirit that permeates this book.

I want to send a heartfelt thank you to everyone who has been a part of the writing journey in some way. This includes James McClellan, Tosha Jones, Rex Hauck, Angela Grant, Karla Winfrey, and Alex Hicks.

Finally, and with deepest gratitude, I thank God for the path that led me to this book. I never thought that I would say this, but the trials and tribulations I've faced have been the crucible in which these words were forged. Through them, I've learned invaluable lessons that I hope will resonate with all who learn of my story.

INTRODUCTION

At 30 years old, I finally felt like I was where I wanted to be. I was at an exciting point in my career working as a Community Liaison and Program Specialist in the Nashville Mayor's Office, I was pursuing a master's degree in Supply Chain Management at Middle Tennessee State University, and I had a beautiful lady on my arm as I made moves for the future. My heart was full.

It's sometimes hard to fully appreciate the moment when you're young, in the prime of life, and having a blast with your family and best friends. But life was good and the sky was the limit.

My weekends often began with hanging out in downtown Nashville with my "Dunnies." That's how my closest friends and I referred to each other. It was our Southern twist on the New York term of endearment "Dun Son" that young men used to greet one another. My cousin, Decosta, my childhood friends, Tracy, JW, Theo, King, Nick, Tremayne, Deon, and a host of others were my Dunnies. If we missed each other on Fridays, we often spent Saturdays enjoying brunch and patronizing local bars and restaurants. That was our thing. My boys and I did this to connect with people around the city and to stay connected with each other. Our outings famously became known as "Sushi Saturdays."

I often had people over to my home where we hung out for hours. My next-door neighbor and childhood friend, Reggie P., opened his home to the gatherings and we would have a two-home shindig. These events made for some great times and memories.

I always tried to fit in a workout on weekends. I loved playing in pickup basketball games and working out in the circuit training area at the local gym. Exercise was not only a way for me to stay in shape, but it had its social advantages as well. I met a lot of people, including local businessmen, and even worked out with a few Tennessee Titans football players. I enjoyed the networking, comradery, and attention that came with being in these settings. I was relatively known and could fit in socially in any circle with little effort. Everywhere my friends and I went, we seemed to have little trouble and much respect.

On Sunday mornings, I took my place in the audio/visual room at church where I controlled the cameras and assisted with sound and lighting. My older brother, Pastor Darrell A. Drumwright, was the minister at The Temple Church and I always felt better after hearing him speak.

It was my friends and family who helped me keep things in perspective. My two brothers and I were inseparable. My little brother, David, and I bonded over music and making tracks. As kids, we joined in as Darrell played the piano and sang anything from gospel to pop radio hits. Music had always been a passion for all three of us. It was a safe way of expression, and we just so happened to have the talent.

My weekends were always complete when I made it to see my doll, Brandy. We often spent time with her seven-year-old son going to local events, eating out, and hanging with friends and family. When we weren't feeling as adventurous, we spent evenings at home watching movies, cooking dinner, chilling out, or doing whatever we felt like doing in the moment.

On Monday mornings, it was back to work at the Mayor's Office. Among many other things, our department acted as a liaison between the mayor and various agencies of the city government, and we regularly helped residents who were in need. For example, we would connect a constituent who had trouble paying their electric bills with a program that had emergency funds to ensure families could keep their lights on. I liked my job. I was involved in many initiatives that really helped people. I was also able to network with people in prominent positions, which could do nothing but help me advance in my endeavors. Also, it sounded pretty cool saying I worked for the mayor.

As a kid, I remember hearing my grandmother say, "Life's a journey, take the trip." Those words have always stayed with me, and I was enjoying my journey to the max.

***

In my quiet moments, I sat on my back patio and looked over the lake and trees that led up to the back yard. It was the perfect place to have conversations with myself as I took a long drag from a square – a single cigarette I occasionally picked up at the corner store on my way home. On pleasant afternoons, the sun shined through the trees and reflected off the water. It was a beautiful sight. I loved how the sun warmed my skin and the smell of the outdoors. I often walked to the lake front, which was but feet from my condo, to listen to the water and nature. I even loved being outside at night, listening to the outdoor sounds and admiring the night sky. While I may have appeared more high-maintenance and interested in popular culture from the outside, I considered myself diverse and well-rounded. I engaged in the city's vast social scene, but being connected to the simple things in life – nature, spirituality, and me time – were also important to me.

I often pondered about where I was on my life path. On the surface, it seemed like I had it all together, but when the layers were peeled back, I was exposed. As a diabetic since childhood, I tried to manage my condition with diet and exercise, but I also had some bad habits. I smoked a little more than I should, especially when I got stressed out. I didn't check my blood sugar level as much as I should. I missed too many appointments with my primary care physician who kept me on track with my diabetes check-ups. I had unresolved issues from my past – like the death of my mother when I was in high school and a complex relationship with my father – that occasionally haunted my present. And when I experienced my darkest days – physically and spiritually – it made me question if life was worth living at all.

I was challenged to view myself and the world in new ways. I was forced to re-examine and redefine my understanding of "manhood," "strength," "faith," and "success."

At the end of the day, I was committed to accepting the consequences for my actions and learning from my mistakes. Even though I tried to make the best decisions for my life, sometimes I fell short. I knew I couldn't control my every circumstance, but I could choose how I would respond to them. I can't say that I was completely at peace with not being in control. But, I learned to work hard for what I wanted, influence what I could, and the rest was out of my hands. I learned to have faith that God is the only one Who has full control.

This is a thought that started to come into full view in November 2014 when I began to simultaneously experience the best and worst 12 months of my entire life. It's amazing the difference a day, a week, a month can make.

Day 1 — November 25, 2014

The holidays are a busy and festive time of year for most people; I was no exception. Not only did my family have large gatherings for Thanksgiving and Christmas, there were also plenty of work and social gatherings to attend. It was also the season that I celebrated my birthday. I typically didn't make a big deal about my birthday, but Brandy wanted to change all that. This particular year, she and I planned a vacation to Las Vegas to commemorate my day. I was looking forward to the opportunity to get away and enjoy some one-on-one time with my doll.

As we prepped for our trip, I had several tasks to check off my list before leaving town, including a visit to the eye doctor. I had been experiencing blurry vision and excess water in my right eye for a couple of months and was scheduled for an outpatient procedure to correct the issue.

My eye had started out as a small nuisance with me noticing a little bit of fuzziness in my vision as I went about my daily routine; then, it gradually got worse. For instance, while driving, objects that were up close as well as objects down the road all appeared blurry. After several appointments, my doctor finally diagnosed me with retina inflammation – a condition that I was told was fixable with proper medical care. I wasn't terribly worried. Doctors' offices were not foreign territory for me, as I was regularly examined, poked and prodded during appointments related to my diabetes since the age of 14. I had never experienced any major medical complications, and I didn't expect to have any at this visit to the eye doctor.

I opted for a midday appointment because I didn't want to go back to work afterwards. I technically could have gone back to the office, but this was a good excuse to take the afternoon off, chill out, go to the mall, or even get some school work done.

Once in the doctor's office, I got signed-in, completed the insurance paperwork, and checked all the boxes on the patient questionnaire. Then, it was time to see Dr. K., who reviewed scans from my previous visits before I came in that day.

"Well, we've reviewed all the scans and today's injection to suppress the inflammation in your eye should fix your problems," Dr. K. said. "The inflammation is what's been causing the fuzziness in your sight when you try to drive, work and conduct your normal activities."

That was a relief to hear that this annoyance would soon be eliminated. Before I'd received an official diagnosis from Dr. K., I didn't know what to make of what was going on. Through my internet research, I found that different things can cause watery eyes, like over-active tear ducts or maybe even allergies.

But once my right eye got so watery that I couldn't see out of it, I knew I had to address the issue before it got worse. I was confident that having this procedure done – at the recommendation of my doctor – was the right thing to do.

The nurse explained what was about to happen next.

"Mr. Drumwright, today we're going to stick a needle in your eye," she said as she began to detail the procedure. "We'll start by applying these numbing drops. And then we'll add some antibacterial drops to prevent infections."

The nurse reclined my seat and inserted metal clips on my right eyelid to hold it back and keep it open. The metal clips were attached to a film that went under my eyelid. I assumed that was to prevent me from blinking while they gave me the shot. I looked up at the light in the ceiling as the procedure began, and as the needle approached my eyeball, the muscles in my body tightened up.

"Don't move, Mr. Drumwright," the nurse said. "You're going to feel the needle when it hits your cornea, but just keep looking directly here," she said as she dangled a small, pen-like object for me to focus on.

One of my biggest fears is having someone put their hands around my neck. There's just something about the threat of being without air that psyches me out. If I see someone's hands coming near my neck, then my first instinct is to put my hands up, block it from happening, and even go as far as wanting to punch whoever is getting that close. I have to say, seeing a 3-inch needle approach my eye gave me the same feeling. And even though I self-administered my insulin shots with a needle, this was very different. But I knew this was a brief, necessary evil I had to endure to get me back to feeling 100 percent and jetting off to an adventure in Vegas with Brandy.

As the needle entered my eye, I thought to myself, Ah, shit! They got me! I don't know what those 'numbing' drops were good for, because they didn't numb ANYTHING!

I suffered in silence. My pride wouldn't let me show much emotion or let on that I was in that much discomfort. I thought it would be a quick ordeal, but it couldn't end soon enough. I was starting to get terrified.

As fluid was pushed into my eye through the needle, the pressure became unbearable. It felt as though they were adding twice the amount of liquid that my eye cavity is supposed to contain. It really hurt. It felt like things were expanding that were not supposed to expand, and it felt like my eye was about to explode.

The weird, pinching pain that I felt in my eyeball didn't last long; maybe 15 minutes. But what followed was different. The pain around my eye – in my temple – is what really hurt, and was the beginning of a throbbing headache that would stick around for the rest of the day.

Following the procedure, the nurses scanned both of my eyes again so the doctor could make sure everything was okay.

"Today's corrective procedure on your right eye went well, Mr. Drumwright," Dr. K said. "I saw a little bit of inflammation on one of the blood vessels on your left eye, but it does not alarm me. We just want to monitor it and catch any future issues that might be similar to what you're currently experiencing with the right eye. The inflammation on your retina is a result of diabetes, but you'll be alright. Your issues will just require proper maintenance. You're a relatively healthy guy; just do what you have to do to manage your condition. You'll also need to get to your primary care physician to make sure everything is okay with your blood sugar levels."

After Dr. K's assessment, I believed that there were no major problems. Yeah, I had something going on that I needed to pay attention to, but it was stuff that was fixable and definitely manageable. The most concerning part of his report is that he told me my condition was diabetes-related. That was shocking and disturbing because I thought I'd been managing my diabetes pretty well, and I had never had these types of issues before. I knew having issues with my eyes was a possibility, but it was not at the forefront of my mind. However, I didn't get too bent out of shape. I focused on all the good that was happening; I was done with needles for the day, my left eye was just fine, and I had a beautiful woman waiting to kick it with me on a birthday getaway. Everything else would have to wait, including my appointment with my primary care doctor who I planned to visit after returning from Vegas.

With nothing more than a headache and some less-than-exciting news about my eyes, I drove myself home and finished getting ready for my trip where I was determined to tune out any negative vibes and turn up the fun. Little did I know I had begun another journey that day that would set my life on a whole new course.

Day 5 — November 29, 2014

As the lights from the Las Vegas Strip illuminated below, the helicopter pilot named David came on over the headset.

"And to the right, you will see the Stratosphere Hotel, Casino and Skypod. You remember us going there in '97, bro?!" the pilot asked. Brandy and I both laughed; his "bro" reference was comical because he shared the same name as my younger biological brother. He knew this was the first time I had returned to Las Vegas since junior high school when my real brother, David, and I left our mark on the city. From the swimming park at the Monte Carlo, to the theme park at Circus Circus, we had a blast. We even visited the spot where legendary rapper Tupac Shakur was killed near the MGM Grand.

Now, I was 30 years old and traveling with my beautiful girlfriend Brandy. My doll and I were "shaking life." We were enjoying a helicopter ride over the city after having dinner at one of Las Vegas' 5-star restaurants.

As we circled the city through the night skies, I watched her peer at the colorful display of lights from the casinos, hotels, and entertainment venues below. Her eyes beamed with excitement and life. Her hair flowed with every turn the helicopter made. She looked amazing. As her eyes turned back toward me, I gazed into them and said, "You are everything."

This would have been a perfect time to pop the big question and make her mine forever. We had been dating for 13 months, and they were some of the best months of my life. I honestly didn't plan on proposing to Brandy in Las Vegas, but I believe that would have been an ideal time to do it. Instead, I had an even bigger vision for a proposal that would include our families and friends. So, I simply pulled her close to me, kissed her lips, felt her hand clinch the chest of my shirt, and enjoyed the moment.

After another few minutes in the air, the helicopter began its descent to the landing pad. Being a goof, I forgot that I was wearing a headset and got tangled up in the cords as I exited the helicopter, another laugh the three of us shared before departing. We enjoyed a few last playful exchanges with the pilot as we made our way inside the office building lobby where the next group awaited its flight.

The night was still young and we took off to a new destination. We had lots of adventures planned while in Vegas, including an all-day trip to the Grand Canyon and a Cirque du Soleil performance. It was the kind of trip you look forward to having with your special someone.

***

While in Vegas, the vision in my right eye began to deteriorate. The blurriness returned, and I began to experience new symptoms. Instead of seeing in-focus images of people near and far, I saw gray figures and eventually what looked like dark shadows of people. At times, I had to close my eye to be able to walk because it was beginning to affect my equilibrium.

According to Dr. K., things were supposed to be better by now, but they were definitely headed in the wrong direction. I officially started to worry and began questioning myself and doubting that a positive outcome was on the horizon.

Was that whole, "we're going to stick a needle in your eye" thing just a waste of time? Because clearly, that procedure did not work, I thought.

What is really going on? Is my diabetes – all of a sudden – causing me problems when I've not had any other real issues before?

I just really gotta get ahead of this and stop missing appointments with my primary care physician. That way, I can have the peace of mind that everything is as it should be.

Even though I was developing feelings of fear, I tried my hardest not to ruin our trip with any bad news. We were creating new memories, and that was my first priority. I would deal with my personal problems another day.

"Brandy, I'm not sure what's going on," I confessed to her. "But I have to go back to the eye doctor as soon as we get back to Nashville."

With her reassuring love, she grabbed my hand and said, "Don't worry, baby. I know it has to be scary. I can only imagine. Just go when we get back and it will all be okay."

***

I knew very early into our courtship that I had found her; "The One." She was fun, loving, and always down for an adventure. Her confidence and good energy filled any room she walked in. Her personality was welcoming and warm, so much so that it gave others confidence. Though I had done well for myself financially, she made me want more and supported me in all my endeavors.

At the time, I didn't know how much a good woman would enrich my life, but it didn't take me long to recognize how special Brandy was.

When you're in a relationship, you tend to mark milestones: like the first date, first kiss, or even the first argument. Brandy and I first met at her son Blake's football game. Tracy, one of my best friends, had a son who played on the same team as Blake. Tracy and I both grew up playing for the legendary UNA Bears youth football team in Nashville, and I was at the game to support the new generation of players. When I saw Brandy, she was wearing an orange and blue UNA jersey with blue jeans. As we passed each other, she smiled and said, "Hello, there."

She was 5 feet 7 inches tall with long hair and honey brown skin. She had a beautiful smile and plenty of personality. I watched from a distance as she cheered on the team from the sideline. She screamed as the team charged onto the field. She even performed a routine along with the cheerleaders. It reminded me of the way my mom and her oldest sister, Maychelle, rooted for their children – me and Decosta respectively – when we played. While Brandy was absolutely stunning that day, I didn't approach her for any substantial conversation.

At that time, I was enjoying the bachelor life. I liked the freedom that came along with being a single man; you get lots of attention from the ladies but there are no concrete obligations that you have to fulfill. I had recently been in a relationship, and I wasn't looking to get back into another one any time soon. I wanted to take some time to focus on personal growth, concentrate on my career advancement, and do all the things that made me happy.

On the flip side, being on the dating scene was a lot of work. And although I didn't think I was ready to commit to one person, I honestly found it more satisfying being with someone I could truly bond with. And deep down, I knew I eventually wanted to share my life with someone one day.

Brandy was beautiful, but I didn't want to get involved with just a pretty face. Not saying I assumed that's all she was, but I didn't want to be disappointed or hurt again. As it turned out, she was more than I could've even prayed for.

As the UNA football season progressed and neared a close, our paths crossed again at the youth championship game. Decosta and I attended the game and we spotted Brandy soon after arriving. Decosta and I gave her the nickname "Gray Pants" because she wore a pair of gray pants that fit like a glove and displayed her flawless figure. That day, we chatted in the bleachers as we watched the boys play in the final contest of the year.

"I missed work to be here," Brandy said. "But it's definitely worth it to see my baby do his thing."

"Oh really? What do you do for a living," I asked as I admired her physical beauty and sweet demeanor.

"I'm a speech therapist," she replied.

Man, was I glad she called out from work! I think I watched her more than I did the game. During our conversation that day, I also learned that she was a year older than me. We knew a lot of the same people and had more in common than I would have thought. She was educated, sharp, and wasn't just out for fun. She seemed to have a good head on her shoulders. I knew I didn't have her all figured out, but I was really impressed by her maturity level and where she was in her profession.

We sometimes reflect on the day we met. She jokes that I "almost missed my blessing" of meeting her, because she wasn't even supposed to be there; she was scheduled to be at work. And I tease her right back suggesting that I probably never would have struck up a conversation with her had it not been for those flattering gray pants she sported.

Ultimately, I believe it was simply meant to be. Brandy was indeed a huge blessing in my life; a partner, friend and supporter. We shared the kind of love – sometimes tough love – and compassion that everyone needs.

Day 9 — December 3, 2014

Fresh off my trip to Vegas, I was experiencing a few mixed emotions. I was still on cloud nine and mentally replaying the best moments of my wonderful weekend with Brandy, but I was a little bummed to be back in the waiting room of my doctor's office so soon. The last procedure was supposed to "fix" the issues with my vision, but it was becoming more obvious every day that my troubles were far from over.

"Fill out these forms and bring them back to the desk when you finish, hun," the receptionist said.

I nodded and had a seat in front of the TV in the waiting area. The news was on, showing the ever-growing traffic problems in Nashville. The new "it" city was growing faster than natives could have ever predicted. Tall buildings were few and far between when I was a child. Now, they were going up faster than toy building blocks. I liked the growth, just not the traffic, which is why I scheduled a 7 a.m. appointment at the eye doctor to beat rush hour. That, and the fact that I couldn't really see out of my right eye. I was the first patient to arrive.

I filled out the questionnaire.

High blood pressure? No.
Heart Disease? No.
Cancer? No.
Diabetes? Yes.

I remember when I first started showing the tell-tale signs of diabetes. My mom noticed that I was drinking fluids excessively and constantly urinating. She was a nurse and very familiar with the symptoms, and a visit to the doctor confirmed I was indeed diabetic. Finding out at a young age was scary, but to my surprise the adjustment wasn't as difficult as I anticipated. I still ate the same things I had always eaten, just in moderation. I stuck to a routine and tried not to over-indulge. My mom made it easier for me because she knew so much about the disease, and she stayed on me about it as well. I felt good about how I'd maintained my condition over the years, however, my recent diagnosis of diabetic-related retina inflammation showed me that I still had more work to do. I hoped that the visit to my doctor this day would put me on a path to healing.

I finished the registration paperwork and returned it to the receptionist. I sat back down and pulled up Instagram – which, at the time, was a newly-popular social media application – on my phone. I scrolled through my feed viewing recent posts. One was a multiple-choice question meant to be a joke from a recent viral news story.

"What is your relationship status? a) Single b) Married c) Legally Blind."

Social media had been flooded with videos of a young woman in Texas named Donna Goudeau and her encounter with news reporters after being arrested for her alleged involvement in a crime. She was identified as the driver of a vehicle used to kidnap and rob a man. Of course, she maintained her innocence, and she had a solid alibi: "I am legally blind," she explained. "They said I drove a getaway car, but I can not see. So, how am I going to drive a car? I'm innocent." When pressed by a reporter if she could see anything at all, Goudeau responded, "Barely!"

The irony of seeing this story after I had driven myself to the eye doctor's office was a hell of a coincidence.

"Daniel Drumwright?" The nurse looked right at me as if to ask if that were my name. In my typical sarcastic fashion, I thought, *Well, I am the only person here.* But, I kept that snarky comment to myself. I got up, we greeted each other with a smile, and then we both headed to a screening room.

"So, you are experiencing vision loss, now?" She asked with a concerned tone.

"Yes, it is pretty much dark. What is going on? Does this happen?" I asked her.

"Not normally, but it has. Let's take some scans." We exited the room and headed toward a blue door at the end of the hallway. Behind the door was a row of three identical machines. She sat me at the first machine and asked me to focus both eyes on a green light in the shape of a star. "Hold still and don't blink," she said while adjusting the machine into the proper position.

A red laser-like line moved from top to bottom. Then, there was a flash. My palms began to sweat as I waited for some abrupt action to happen. "You can sit back," the nurse said.

We exited the room, and she sat me in a much smaller waiting area than the one out front. I pulled out my phone and resumed scanning my Instagram timeline. Not a minute later, the nurse called out to me.

"Mr. Drumwright, we're ready."

The nurse and I entered another room where I would meet with the doctor. As I sat in the examination chair, she pulled up my scans on the computer. I tried to sneak a peek at the pictures without being obvious, and then the door opened. It was Dr. K.

"Mr. Drumwright, very nice to see you again. You're here a week early, though. What's going on?" I had a routine post-procedure check-up appointment scheduled for the following week, but I had decided I didn't want to wait that long. I exhaled and uttered my concerns to Dr. K.

"It's my right eye. I can't see. Is this normal?" I asked him.

"Well, it does happen from time to time," he responded in a calm tone. "Let's look at the scans."

He pulled up the images and began to make his assessment.

"The blood flow in your eyes has actually improved quite a bit. Everything is looking okay," he reported.

I was immediately relieved. I asked, "Then, what do I need to do?"

"Just allow it to heal," the doctor responded. "Come in next week and we will do a minor laser procedure on your left eye. Nothing big. This will be just a preventative measure to keep the blood vessels in that eye from having any leaks or issues. You are doing okay."

I smiled and nodded. I was happy nothing seemed to be a huge concern. And yet, I wasn't fully at peace, either. After all, I couldn't see out of my right eye. However, I decided to listen to my doctor and not worry myself. As I prepared to depart Dr. K's office, I scheduled my next appointment for the following Tuesday.

I left my appointment and was eager to call Brandy. I knew she'd be happy about the news. I opened my phone, swiped the screen and was met by the Instagram post I was viewing when I was called back to the examination room.

Legally blind. I shook my head at the thought. As comical as that whole Donna Goudeau story was, it wasn't funny to me at that moment. It was serious. It was real. When I saw the story before my doctor visit, it was entertaining because it was far-fetched and didn't seem like reality. Now, it was starting to hit close to home. I closed my IG account and proceeded to make my call.

"Hey baby. How did the appointment go?" Brandy asked.

"It went okay," I assured her.

"Good. What did he say?" she asked.

I went on to explain what the doctor concluded.

"So glad you feel better now," Brandy said. She was just getting to work and couldn't talk long.

"Yeah. It's crazy, but I'm just gonna let the doctors do their part and I'll do mine," I said with confidence.

"Okay baby. Well, I gotta get to work. You got enough vision to make it to my place tonight, right?" she asked with hints of sarcasm and humor.

"Barely!" I replied with a huge grin. She erupted with laughter. That's the kind of relationship we had. Fun and full of life. She was happy that I was no longer overly stressed about the circumstance and had a bit of my usually goofy personality back. And, although I was having trouble with my eyes, I was still very independent, driving myself to and from the doctor, work, or anywhere else I needed to go. And with my 7 a.m. appointment out of the way, I proceeded to make my way to the office.

***

I got on the road, hoping traffic wasn't bad, but it was awful, as usual. I decided to take the bypass that routed me around the traffic and took me past the exit that led to my previous employer, the Tennessee Lottery. I really enjoyed that job. The people were great and the atmosphere was positive. However, I was presented with a chance to advance my career that I couldn't pass up.

One Fall morning, I received a call from my Aunt Brenda who had worked in government for many years.

"Hey, Daniel. There's an opportunity at the Mayor's Office that I think you would be perfect for," she said with delight.

I was offered the job of community liaison and program specialist after a successful interview with Mayor Karl Dean. I was so excited, but leaving my job at The Lottery was tough. I had made several great relationships, but I had to be open to change to achieve my long-term aspirations of a highly-successful career.

I finally navigated traffic and reached the office. Work was relaxed. There were no scheduled meetings or initiatives to work on that day. No one had an appointment to see Mayor Dean, so he was in the field attending holiday events. Preparing the invitations for our upcoming holiday luncheon and Quarterly Neighborhoods Captains' meeting was my only priority. I helped prepare the agenda, rehearsed my presentation, and took constituent calls.

I headed to the office kitchen where coffee and cookies awaited whomever wanted to indulge. I flavored my coffee with two creams and three packs of sweetener. I said hello to coworkers and staff as I made my way back down to what Erin, my co-worker, and I referred to as The Dungeon. The "Front Line" is what we joked our main job was. My phone was ringing as I approached my desk.

"Mayor's Office of Neighborhoods. This is Daniel speaking."

Day 11 — December 5, 2014

The remainder of the week flew by and before I knew it, it was Friday afternoon. I hadn't noticed any improvement in my right eye all week, but I decided to try to enjoy my weekend and not worry about it. Brandy texted me as I drove home from work.

"Let's just stay in tonight. We can grab takeout for dinner and watch a movie," she wrote. I was perfectly fine with that. We had been planning to go to a holiday gathering, but we were both still catching our breath from our Vegas trip and the work week. I had been feeling fatigued and a bit under the weather since returning, so staying in was preferred that night.

I stopped at the condo I shared with my dad and brother to grab a change of clothes for the following day. I picked up food from a neighborhood casual dining chain and headed to Brandy's home. I used the spare garage door opener she had given me to let myself in, and I was greeted by a goofy and rambunctious seven-year-old, Blake, who was eager to show off his dance moves.

He jumped out from hiding behind the wall, and started pop-locking and gyrating in the middle of the room like it was his own personal dancefloor. His moves mimicked the popular choreography of Mindless Behavior, a young boy group whose members had pretty boy, hip-hop style.

"Hey, Poot Cookie," he said to me after finishing his dance. Poot Cookie was a term I made up, and it was just another way that Blake and I picked at each other.

"Hey Diet Poot Cookie!" I replied. Then, I went in for the one-handed lift. I picked him up and held him over my head, as I cheerfully said silly jokes like, "Boy, I'm going to get you. I'm going to toss you up right through this ceiling!"

Just like his mom, Blake had a big personality and was always ready for fun. I felt being a jokester was his way of breaking the ice and getting attention without having to let his guard down or be too vulnerable. I noticed that very early on in our relationship. I understood it and used that to connect with him. I loved jokes, too, and I knew it was a way of being comfortable in sometimes uncomfortable situations.

I carried my bag and gym clothes upstairs. I had planned on playing in a basketball game that weekend, but with my vision issues I would have to settle for a weekend workout. When I entered the room, Brandy was there unpacking the last of her suitcase. I walked up to her from behind and pulled her in close before giving her a kiss on her neck. I admired her as I looked at her reflection in the bedroom mirror.

"Hello, beautiful," I said as I began to dance with her. Blake walked in and rolled his eyes. We all sat on the bed and ate our food. I ate a salmon Caesar salad, my usual. It was a wet and windy night, so after we finished eating, we all got under the sheets and fell asleep while watching a movie.

**

The first time I met Blake was a night that Brandy invited me to dinner at her house. Blake's plans with his dad for the weekend had fallen through and Blake was unexpectedly home for the weekend. Although Brandy was reluctant to have me in her house and around her son so early in our relationship, she took a chance and invited me over anyway. So, I came over and Blake was instructed to stay upstairs while we had dinner.

While Brandy and I were watching TV, she received a phone call and was briefly distracted. While she was talking, I heard the steps creaking. Sure enough, it was Blake peeking around the corner.

I looked up at him and gave him a "bro nod," our non-verbal way of saying, "What's up, bruh." Blake flashed a quick smile at me and quietly walked back upstairs. He was being nosy trying to figure out who was downstairs with his momma.

About an hour later, Brandy and I finished our meal, and she expressed her surprise that Blake had been M.I.A. all night. "I'm surprised Blake hasn't come down here yet," she said.

"Well, he peeked down here a little while ago from the top of the stairs. I saw him," I informed her.

"Oh, he did?" Brandy asked. "Well, I'll tell him to come down here now." She called his name, and Blake came bouncing down the stairs.

"This is mister Blake," Brandy said as she introduced us.

"I remember you from the football game, buddy. What's good?" I responded.

"What's up, man?" he said in a polite and almost skeptical tone.

Like many male conversations, we didn't have to exchange many words. But we both extended a welcoming vibe to one another, and that was enough for me to know that things between us would be cool.

When I was courting Brandy, Blake was present during many of my visits. It was very easy for me to include him. Whether it was going outside to ride bikes, getting something to eat, or going to the movies, Blake was a part of Brandy's life, so he was naturally becoming a part of mine. I always wanted him to know that he didn't have to be biologically mine for me to love him. Brandy never pressured me to forge a relationship with Blake, but I thought, *why wouldn't I?* For me, I didn't want to be "that guy" who only wanted to spend time with the mom and not her son. I guess she didn't want me to feel that Blake was my responsibility, initially. Maybe she was testing me, seeing if I could be invested in both of them.

Four months into our relationship, Brandy, Blake and I were hanging out when she asked him, "You like Daniel, don't you?"

"He's cool," Blake responded.

"You think I'm cool enough to stick around for a while?" I asked him.

"Ummm…I think so. As long as you don't be acting crazy, because then I'll have to beat you," he joked.

From that point on, we became comfortable with one another organically.

"Boy, whatever," I replied. "You couldn't break wind."

Day 15 — December 9, 2014

Tuesday morning arrived and my appointment for the preventative laser procedure on my left eye was at 12:15 p.m. So, I took a half-day off from work. I was a little unsettled because my vision had not improved.

"Are you worried about your appointment?" Brandy asked.

"I'm good, baby," I said as I tried to sound more confident than I actually was. "I know I have to do it, so I'm just gonna get through it. We still on for lunch?"

"Absolutely," she replied as she kissed me goodbye. "Call when you're headed to your appointment."

It was hard enough having diminished sight in my right eye; adding an elective procedure to the left eye was even more nerve-racking. But, if my doctor was right, and this would keep the blood vessels in my "good" eye from displaying complications from my diabetes like leaks or inflammation, then it was worth it.

Dr. K was in a jolly mood when I arrived at his office that morning. Although I was there for a procedure on my left eye, I asked him to make a quick observation of my right eye before proceeding. Whistling and bobbing his head, he reviewed my previous eye scans and I leaned forward to be examined.

"Your right eye has normal scarring. Everything should start to correct itself. I don't see any cause for concern," he said. "The vision in your right eye hasn't gotten any better yet?"

I shook my head, "No."

"Don't get too discouraged," he said. "We'll just give it some time."

"So, what should I expect from this procedure on my left eye today?" I asked nervously.

He put his hand on my shoulder to assure and comfort me.

"You will feel a little discomfort as the laser hits your retina. You'll also experience a bit of blurriness immediately after the procedure, but it should subside after 24 to 48 hours," the doctor said as he ducked behind his equipment. The machine resembled the scopes used to test a patient's vision, except it had red laser lights beaming from the head mount. I reluctantly leaned in so the doctor could set the machine's sights on treating the area of concern. As anxious as I was, I was relieved to know I was doing what was necessary to fix and prevent any future issues.

We finished up, and as I was told, there was obvious blurriness, but nothing I couldn't deal with. I headed to meet Brandy for lunch at Chili's near her job. Of course, she asked all about the visit. I spoke confidently about the procedure, but I was still concerned. I couldn't put my finger on it, but an eerie feeling had overcome me.

Was everything actually 'normal,' and was there really no cause for concern like Dr. K said?

"You headed home for the day?" she asked as we finished our meal.

"Yeah, I'm just going to go home and relax," I said. "Maybe finish my last final exam for school so I can be done until next semester. Just call me when you get off."

She kissed me long and hard. "Everything is fine," she assured me as I opened her car door, helped her in, and watched as she pulled off.

***

I planned on finishing my last grad school exam since I had the afternoon off from work, but I couldn't focus long enough to complete it. I went home, sat on my back patio, and smoked a cigarette. Smoking wasn't an everyday habit for me, but the stress was mounting and I needed one. I was juggling a lot: grad school, a new relationship, a full-time job, and an active social life with my friends and church family. And now, these unexpected health struggles had the potential of putting a strain on all of these things. Without good health, unfortunately, everything else was in jeopardy. For the first time in my life, I felt like I almost had everything going for me. Then, all this started.

As much as I enjoyed the scenery in my back yard, I could not relax. I was looking for some reassurance. So, I closed my eyes and struck up a conversation.

"God, thank you for getting me to the doctor to get all of this taken care of. This is the last thing I thought I would be dealing with, but thank you."

I hit the half-smoked square and looked at it. I was mad at myself for even picking up another cigarette. I tossed it over the balcony and watched it hit the ground below.

Daniel, stop worrying, I said to myself as I got a hold of my emotions. You're just dealing with a setback. Stop letting this plague your mind. I could worry myself sick, but what good would that do? I felt silly for being so worried.

I opened the sliding door to go back inside. As I turned around to lock the door, I covered my left eye, to completely blind myself. I laughed and smiled. As scary as it was, there was no way I was going blind.

I gathered myself long enough to finish my final exam and called it an early night so that I could prepare for the next workday and my diabetes check-up the following morning.

Day 16 — December 10, 2014

I rose early the next morning and the blurriness in my left eye from the laser procedure had subsided. My vision was back to normal in my left eye. I arrived at my primary care physician's office for my appointment, and the nurse did her normal routine. She checked my weight and blood pressure, took me to get my blood work, got my urine sample, and showed me to the examination room.

Dr. Wolfe, my PCP and diabetes specialist, entered the room with her face turned up at me. "You finally decided to come in," she said calling me out. "Your blood sugar is 243. Did you eat this morning?"

I hadn't eaten and was surprised to hear it was that high. I had, however, noticed my blood sugars were running higher than normal for about a month or so. As I started to have issues with my vision, I began checking my blood sugar levels about twice a day. Dr. Wolfe preferred that I did it even more frequently than that. She suggested three to five times a day. I used a lancet – a small needle needed to quickly pierce my finger and get a few drops of blood – and a glucose test strip. While a normal blood glucose level for someone without diabetes is about 90 to 99 mg/dL, an alarming number to me was anything over 200. My doctor, however, was concerned with anything at 180 and above. I had Type 1, juvenile-onset diabetes. That meant I was insulin dependent. So, I used a syringe to pull insulin through a vial and administered a shot in my belly twice a day.

I thought about how my energy level had slumped over the past few months. I wrote it off, because I had been on the go. Trying to manage my busy schedule, I wasn't paying attention to how tired I actually was. The thought never crossed my mind that my fatigue could be due to elevated blood glucose levels. However, with my recent vision issues and my sparse self-monitoring, I began questioning if I'd been managing my diabetes as well as I thought.

Before I could reply she stated, "Your weight and blood pressure are good, but I'm going to need you to monitor your sugars better."

I knew telling her about my recent eye procedures would really get her going. Dr. Wolfe had been my primary care physician since I was 18 years old. My aunt took me to see her after my mother passed away and I had been going to her ever since. I told her about my eye procedures with the needle and the laser, and we simply talked about life in general.

"You have to make sure you are on top of this," she advised me. "You have a lot of things going for you, Daniel. And you've done a good job taking care of yourself, besides missing your appointments with me. Sounds like you have a good woman on your side and you have to make sure you are able to take care of her."

Everything she said to me made sense. And everything she said was right. Everything. She wrote my new prescriptions and told me the nurse would contact me with my blood work results in a few days.

I wasn't feeling any better, but I looked forward to putting all this doctor stuff behind me and getting back to normalcy.

Day 25 — December 19, 2014

Fridays were rarely busy at work, and because it was the Friday before Christmas Day, the office was dead. I was the first person in the office that morning. The day eased by smoothly and I found myself searching for things to keep me busy until closing time. I was looking forward to being off work for a couple of weeks during the holidays and not returning to the office until after the New Year.

About an hour before leaving work, my cell phone rang. I recognized the number as my primary care physician's office.

"Mr. Drumwright. We just wanted to call and give you some information from your appointment," the nurse began.

I expected this call from my doctor's nurse. It had been two days since my visit which is about the length of time it generally took to receive lab results from the various tests I underwent. However, this time the call took an unexpected turn.

"Your A1C – your blood sugar – was a little elevated the day we drew your blood. But most importantly, your white blood cell count was abnormally high."

Not sure what to make of that report, I started asking questions. "Okay. What does white blood cell count mean?" I inquired.

"Well, we don't want to scare you, but…"

Any time a medical professional says, "we don't want to scare you," it's an automatic trigger for getting scared! So, of course, I was immediately spooked.

"We are going to refer you to a specialist who deals with blood disorders," the nurse continued. "An elevated white blood cell count can be caused by a number of things. So, instead of speculating a bunch of different scenarios, we want to send you to an oncologist." They scheduled an appointment for me at Tennessee Oncology for January 5. So, unfortunately, I would have to wait another 17 days for answers.

In the moment, I didn't think much about the type of doctor that an oncologist is – essentially, a cancer doctor. I was mostly just frustrated that, once again, I was being referred to *another* doctor. I had already undergone two eye procedures, been to seven doctor appointments within 30 days, and I was starting to feel a loss of control. I was trying my best to get back to normal but it wasn't happening. I started to accept that there was something deeper going on with my health that had not been readily apparent a month ago.

A feeling of helplessness came over me, and I began to wonder if there was anything I could do to fix my situation. All I could do was follow the doctor's orders that I was being given and show up at the next appointment. I couldn't substitute a workout at the gym for a doctor visit and expect that to make my white blood cell count better. I couldn't eat a salad and expect my blood sugar to be okay. There was no one I could call, no where I could go, or nothing I could do to change my circumstance. I had no control.

This shit sucks, was the most dominant thought in my head.

The call from the nurse lasted only a few minutes. After we hung up, I quickly did an online search of the phrase "elevated white blood cell count" to see what potential causes I could find. There was a lot of content there, but I decided not to self-diagnose my condition based on internet searches. Instead, I called Brandy to fill her in on the news I had just received.

"Damn, why am I going through all this?" I said to her with an exasperated spirit.

Brandy quickly tried to ease my concerns. "Do they know what is causing your white blood cell count to spike? Do you think that may be the cause of your eye issues?" she asked, hoping to gain a better understanding.

"I'm not sure," I replied. "That's why they are sending me to a specialist."

She could tell I was worried and decided not to ask me any more questions.

"Baby, just forget about it for now, and don't stress yourself any more than you already are. I'm so sorry you are going through all this. Just go to the next appointment, and hopefully, you will get all the answers and put this behind you."

I didn't say anything in response. I just sat looking at my computer screen.

"Daniel, you okay?" She sounded more uneasy and almost afraid.

I quickly assumed a guarded posture, covering up my concerns with confidence, and gave her an optimistic response. "I'm okay. Just trying to make sense of this. Don't worry yourself, either."

We ended the conversation so that we could both finish our workday. I wanted to find something to keep my mind from wandering to a place of anxiety and fear. Since there wasn't much work to be done at the office that day, I pulled out my laptop to work on a few music tracks. I placed the headphones over my ears and vibed to the music. It was an up-tempo track that my brother, David, and I had been tweaking for a while.

As much as I tried to distract myself with music at that moment, I couldn't stay focused because the phone call from the nurse really shook me.

I left work early and prepared to start my weekend. When I got home, I packed a bag and got myself ready to go out with my Dunnies. As I made my way into the hallway, I noticed my dad walking out the front door.

"Hey, where you headed?" I asked.

"Oh, I'm headed to eat with my lady."

I figured he would be gone for the evening, so I rushed downstairs to give him a hug. "I'll be staying with Brandy for the weekend, so I'll see you Sunday night."

Not long after my father departed, I grabbed my insulin from the refrigerator and headed out the front door. The weather was unusually warm for a winter day, so I let the top down on my car and headed downtown.

***

As usual, the evening with my boys was fun. We all had a few beverages and talked for hours about everything, including our plans for the approaching New Year. I took this opportunity to share some exciting news.

"Yeah, this will probably be the last New Year's I have as a true bachelor," I said aloud. None of them were surprised. Brandy and I had been dating for about 14 months, and they knew I was crazy about her. I pulled out my cell phone and held up a picture of a diamond ring.

A month before this outing with my friends, I visited a jeweler at the mall on my lunch break. I knew Brandy's ring size, the type of ring she preferred and I was ready to take our relationship to the next level. I paid cash for the engagement ring and wedding band in one transaction. The engagement ring had a princess cut center piece diamond with four smaller diamonds on each side with a white gold band. The wedding band was white gold encrusted with small diamonds on the top half of the band.

All my Dunnies were happy for me, though they gave me a hard time.

"Bro, you must know, you are about to throw in all your cards, for real!" Theo teased me.

"You got the ring, Dunny?! Yeah, it's over. You're about to give it all up!" JW chimed in.

Like most close friends, we could pick at each other and know that it was nothing but love. I needed that, considering how worried I was about my sight and health. If there was anything I was sure of, it was Brandy. I had never gotten close to this point with anyone else, but our relationship just felt right.

At the end of the night, my Dunnies and I settled up our checks, said our goodbyes, and went our separate ways. As I left, I couldn't ignore the scary things that were happening to me, and my thoughts were plagued with "what ifs."

What if my sight completely fails me and I can't keep working?

What if I can't support a wife and child?

What if Brandy decides that this is too much of a burden to weigh herself down with?

What if this health battle is the life challenge that breaks my faith?

Even more concerning, I was starting to see a glare in my vision from car headlights while I was driving home at night. With diminished sight and the effect of the adult beverages I had at the bar starting to set in, I didn't need any more problems. I said to myself, Let's get in the far-right lane and set this cruise control. I made it to Brandy's home, where she and Blake were waiting for me.

"Hey, how was it? Did y'all have fun?" Brandy asked as I made my way in.

"Yeah, it was fun. You know how we do," I replied.

I couldn't reveal all the details of our conversations. She had no idea that I was in the beginning stages of preparing a surprise of a lifetime for her.

We made our way upstairs and got ready for bed. Before falling asleep, Brandy rolled over and stated that she, in fact, had a surprise of her own. Despite being completely exhausted, I was intrigued by the idea that she was planning something for us. Before I could even ask for a hint or make a guess, she grabbed me and squealed, "We're getting a dog!"

I wasn't exactly excited to hear this, since she really didn't get my opinion before making the decision. I didn't oppose the idea, though. I loved dogs. So, I just offered one of my typical sarcastic replies.

"Well, I wasn't prepared to give Blake a sibling before we tie the knot."

Day 26 — December 20, 2014

The next morning, Blake, Brandy and I woke up and prepared for the hour-long trip to get the puppy. After persistently searching advertisements online and in local newspapers, Brandy found out about a litter of Yorkshire Terriers in Franklin, Tennessee. Having pets was Brandy's thing, and she was a serial dog lover. She almost always had a dog in her life since the age of seven. To her, pets were comforting. She grew up as an only child, and Blake was the only child of an only child. So naturally, he was thrilled about the idea of getting a dog. The puppy would be Blake's Christmas gift, and we both thought it might give Blake a sense of responsibility as well as a little companionship.

My vision was noticeably blurry, but I got dressed and hoped my vision would clear up as the day progressed. Instead of saying anything about it, and possibly bringing down the joyful mood, I proceeded as I would any other day.

When we arrived at our destination, we were greeted by a young girl and a litter of Yorkies. "Granny, they're here!" the girl said as she opened the door. We entered and spoke with an older lady who was excited to introduce us to the puppies and their parents. I could sense the excitement from both the puppies and Brandy.

I turned to Brandy as she stated, "There she is!" Trailing the crew of dogs was the runt of the litter. We left the home with the smallest and liveliest puppy of them all. But like the old saying goes, it's "not the size of the dog in the fight, but the size of the fight in the dog." We would learn that Minx was a feisty girl, very territorial and protective of Brandy.

"Can we name her Minx?" Brandy asked. Minx was the only girl dog and that's what Brandy wanted. She was cute, but among the three of us, I was the least excited about the dog. Blake recently had a gerbil named Dirty Blanco who should have been named Houdini. He escaped from his cage more times than I can remember. I eventually set him free after he chewed through a hose under the kitchen sink and nearly flooded the downstairs. This, plus I just had so much going on that getting a pet was the least of my concerns. But I went along with it because it made my lady and Blake happy.

I replied, "Welcome home, Minx," as we made our way back to Nashville.

All the while, I was nervous and anxious to get to the oncologist. A dog was a somewhat nice way to divert my attention from the condition of my vision which seemed to be deteriorating more and more. Attempting to return to some sense of normalcy, I tried to focus on enjoying the holidays and all the joy they bring.

***

Day 31 — December 25, 2014

I got up early on Christmas morning and headed to the kitchen. I had decided to make breakfast and invite my father and Brandy's mother to join us. My vision was quite blurry and the daylight from outside seemed to cause an unbearable glare. Despite that, I was looking forward to a lovely day. The house was decked out in full Christmas décor. The stockings were hung, the holiday lights were strung, gifts were tucked under the Christmas tree waiting to be opened, and everyone woke up to a prepared meal, including Minx. After breakfast, Blake's father came to visit, drop off gifts, and help Blake set up his new scooter. It was a nice morning.

That afternoon, I went to my condo to grab a few things before heading to my aunt's home for Christmas dinner. I had to strain my eyes to see while I was driving, and that caused me to have a headache. So, I was looking forward to riding with David for the rest of the night.

While I was getting dressed for dinner, specks in my vision that were hard to see through began to appear. I was notorious for acting like things didn't bother me, but this was hard to ignore. I did my best to carry on as usual and not raise any alarms. I was ready to go before David, so I sat on the front porch by myself until he made his way outside. He lit up a cigarette as we walked toward my car.

"Hey Daniel, that grille on the front of your car looks good!" he said with admiration in his voice. Days earlier, I had installed a chrome grille on my matte black, 2009 convertible Chrysler Sebring. It was my Christmas gift to myself. I ordered it online and put it on right there in the parking lot of my condo. I was excited to see how nice it made my car look, and the young Latino boy who lived next door told me, "I love your car, Mr. Daniel. It looks like a race car!" I imagined myself, Brandy, Blake, and Minx riding down the highway with the top down enjoying the wind blowing through our hair. My daydream was a much clearer picture than the vision I was actually experiencing.

"You might have to let me whip it around town sometime," David said.

I didn't want to spend the rest of the day with a headache from straining my eyes to drive, so I tossed him my keys.

"Go ahead. Drive it now and save your gas," I replied. Casually inviting David to drive was a convenient way for me to disguise how much I was really struggling. I didn't want to tell him the whole truth about what was going on with me, and I figured he would love the opportunity to push my whip.

I always felt responsible for David because he was the youngest. Watching over my baby brother was the first job I had. He was only 15 years old when we lost our mom, and there was nothing I could do to protect him from that. There were times when I wasn't there for David the way that I should have been, though.

Not because I was a bad big brother, but simply because I wasn't there when he needed me. One incident in particular was when he was shot in the back of the head with a pellet gun. I can remember coming home from baseball practice, and my mom telling me.

He was fine, but we knew the kid who did it so I was out to get him. For weeks, I rode around the neighborhood on my bike hoping to find him. He and his twin brother had moved and only occasionally visited the area to stay with their grandmother, but I was determined to whoop his ass. I never found him, though. I vowed that I would never let anyone mess with David like that again. Though David was a Black Belt and could fend for himself, he was never going to have to worry about me having his back. Now that I was having medical issues of my own, I tried to hide the severity of my condition from him and protect him from being burdened and worried about me.

We walked to the car, David popped the trunk and threw my bag inside. As he closed the trunk he asked, "So, how is your sight now?"

He didn't realize it, but a feeling of uneasiness and worry was in my spirit. Even though the eye doctor kept telling me he saw nothing that was a cause for concern, my vision continued to worsen.

"David, I don't know what is going on, but I'm beginning to worry. My vision keeps getting blurrier. I keep going to different doctors, and… Man, I'm just ready for this to be over," I said trying to hold back tears. He reached for my arm and looked at me. He didn't say anything immediately, but his look and embrace gave me comfort. As he pulled me close, I began to weep. He dropped his half-finished cigarette and said, "It's okay. If you need me to, I'll take you to the doctor's office Monday. Let's just get through the weekend."

On the ride to my aunt's house, I looked around at everything we passed. The ride had become so familiar over the years that I could close my eyes and almost know exactly where I was. As we passed The Hermitage, where President Andrew Jackson lived, I thought of school trips there as a child. I wanted to remember every detail of everything I had seen or done. In front of me, I saw a Tennessee Titans license plate on an old Caprice Classic. It brought back memories of my mother rooting for Steve McNair and Eddie George on Sunday afternoons. I was beginning to feel like these memories were the kind you get when you are nearing death, so I quickly snapped myself out of it and turned the music up.

We eventually pulled up to my aunt's house, and dinner was in full swing. We were greeted at the door by our brother, Darrell, and our sister-in-law, Tonya. We made our way around the house greeting everyone and telling them "Merry Christmas." The men were upstairs in the den watching the NBA Christmas Day game. My male cousins were arguing about whether LeBron or Kobe was closer to Jordan in greatness. The teens were in the computer room watching the movie *Friday After Next*. The women were downstairs reminiscing on their early years. It was Christmas dinner like always. We spent a few hours talking, eating, and catching up before David needed to leave.

"Hey, are you ready to head out?" David asked me as he put on his coat. "I know dad is still chilling, so you can just drop me off at the crib so I can get my car." I looked out the door and saw the sun had nearly set. My dad was not quite ready to go and I knew I was supposed to get to Brandy's house soon. So, I gathered my things and said goodbye to everyone.

As we made our way outside, it was evident that it wasn't safe for me to drive. Everything looked dim with the lack of sunlight and the street lights caused a glare in my vision. Still, I got in the driver's seat and started the car. I sat there wondering if my vision would get better soon. The thought that I might be going blind lingered in my mind and began to make me nervous. I didn't want to seem worried, so I looked at David and said, "You know, I think I'm gonna stay a little longer. I'll just ride home with Daddy and use one of his cars if I need to leave."

Surprised, David asked if I was sure. I was surer than I let him know. I gave him a hug and told him to be safe and take care of my car. As he pulled off, I called Brandy.

"Hey baby! Are you headed this way?" she asked, sounding as if she knew I was on the way.

"Brandy, I'm sorry. I can't come," I said with a shaky voice.

"Why not? Are you too lit?" I could tell there was some disappointment in her voice.

I exhaled and began to explain. I told her that, while I was willing to drive across town to see her, I was just uneasy about being behind the wheel in my condition.

There was a brief silence. I could hear her family's voices in the background as they enjoyed themselves. I didn't want it to seem like I was standing her up or having second thoughts about being with her and her family for the holidays. So, I quickly pivoted.

"Look, I'm going to come. I will just have to be super careful," I said to her.

"No, don't do that," she said right away. "I would hate myself if something happened to you. Promise me you are just... You are being cautious," she said. I reassured her that I was only being safe and wanting nothing more than to be with her and her family. We ended the conversation, and I said a short prayer on my aunt's front steps before returning to the gathering.

Dear God. I don't know what or why this is happening. Please just let this come to an end. Please.

Even when my prayer life wasn't the best and I felt my faith wavering, I had always spoken to God. I had seen Him work in so many circumstances and heard of the many accounts of miracles in people's lives. There was no question in my mind that He existed. I didn't always feel like God gave me exactly what I wanted, but I always got answers to my prayers. And those answers positioned me to obtain more and more of my heart's desires. I truly believed that I had done well by my health, but after the reports from my doctors, I knew I needed to do more. I believed by giving my all to address my mounting health concerns, adding prayer to that effort would yield the positive results that I so desired.

I went back inside my aunt's house and, before I could get comfortable, my dad was ready to go. We fixed to-go plates and told everyone goodbye. We must have been inside longer than I thought, because when I got to the door it was completely dark. I struggled getting to the car. My dad even had to tell me that I was at the back door of his car, instead of the front door.

As we made our way home, the street lights were streaking, almost as if I were watching a time lapse. The headlights from the passing cars created the same blinding glare that the sun caused that morning as I prepared breakfast.

My dad and I arrived at my condo, but I never really got settled in. All I could think about was getting to Brandy. I tried to determine if I could indeed still make it to her aunt's house before their holiday celebration was over. Even though I was very concerned about my vision, I was more concerned with giving everyone the impression that I had flaked out and simply chose not to show up.

I sat on the back patio until I started to nod off.

Day 32 — December 26, 2014

I don't remember coming inside from my patio, but when I awoke, I was on the living room sofa, where I normally fell asleep. It was 7:30 a.m. and I had an unread text from Brandy from the night before. "We made it home. TTYL. Love you," she wrote.

I called her immediately.

"Good morning, Mr. Drumwright. Did you sleep well?" she said as she answered the phone.

"Yeah, I slept okay," I replied happily knowing she wasn't too upset that our plans from the night before did not pan out. She began telling me about her evening and I shared the happenings at my family's gathering.

"Will you be coming over today?" she asked. But really, she was suggesting I had no choice.

"I will be coming with joy!" I responded. We made a plan to go to the movies that night.

"Can you drive?" I asked her with some embarrassment.

She giggled and replied, "If you pay, then I'll drive."

"We have a deal."

As I ended the call, I noticed the tint in my vision was growing more pronounced. It was almost pink. I no longer felt comfortable driving at night, so I had to leave home in plenty of time to get to her place by 5 p.m., about the time when the sun would be completely set. I figured I'd stay with her the whole weekend and be back in the eye doctor's office first thing Monday morning demanding more corrective action.

The doctor keeps saying that I'm okay. I'm not okay. Something's wrong, I thought.

We made it to the movie theater that night to watch "Unbroken." It was a very powerful film about a young Jewish man who was an athlete and former Olympian. He was forced into a life of survival at a concentration camp. Although I was able to follow the storyline, it was an interesting experience attempting to watch a movie while my sight was deteriorating. The picture was fuzzy and there was a huge glare on the screen. When the scenes of the movie were especially bright, a halo or haze appeared in my vision and hindered me from seeing all the visual details.

After the movie, we made our way to the lobby, my eyes did not adjust well to the drastic change in lighting conditions. Leaving the very dark theater, the wall lamps that lined the hall leading outside shined a hazy blue. The lobby was almost painfully bright, and when we stepped outside into the night air, colors appeared flatter and made it difficult for me to navigate the parking lot. Walking outside was like walking into a pit of darkness.

Nevertheless, we made our way home for the evening. It was nice to get out and enjoy each other's company, and take my mind off of my struggles.

Day 33 — December 27, 2014

The following morning, I left Brandy's house to run a few errands. My vision was still quite hazy, but it was better than it had been in some time. I was slightly relieved, until I got to the grocery store. While walking inside, I dropped my car keys on the floor. As I bent over to pick them up, the color red filled the vision in my left eye. It reminded me of how a lava lamp looked as the lava moved like molasses through the clear fluid. In a panic, I rushed through the store to get the few things I needed. I skipped the self-check lanes, because my vision was too bad to check out on my own like I normally did. I approached the nearest cashier and placed the handful of items I had on the conveyor belt.

"How are you doing today, sir?" the young lady at the checkout counter asked.

"Okay," I answered her. But, I wasn't okay. I was far from okay.

I got to the car, rummaged through my bag to find the eye drops I had just purchased, and I applied it to my left eye. I wasn't surprised to find the drops didn't clear up anything. The pink film was much more obvious, and any time I looked down, the red glob moved into my central vision. It was obviously blood, and I grew more frightened. I searched through the contacts in my phone, as well as I could, looking for someone to call. But who? And what would I say? That I was scared and needed assistance just to make a quick run to the grocery store? Logic told me that I needed help, but the thought of actually asking for it made me feel inadequate and slightly embarrassed.

I didn't want to call Brandy and cause her to worry any more than she already had. I didn't want to call my brothers, my dad, or my Dunnies. I didn't want to burden them what a problem that did not have a quick fix. So, I decided not to call anyone, and I drove myself back to Brandy's house.

Brandy, her mom and her cousin had gone shopping at the mall, so the house was empty when I got there. They even took the dog, which I figured was dropped off with Blake at his cousin's home.

I raced to the mirror to see if the red lava in my eye was visible in my reflection. It wasn't. That meant, no one else could see the film; just me. I didn't want to think about anything, so I tried to sleep, but I had no luck.

Everyone arrived back at the house with a few bags and an outfit for the dog. Minx didn't like the clothing and fought to remove the shirt. Brandy and I spent the evening watching TV, and we let Blake play with his toys. I went to sleep not saying anything about what I had experienced at the grocery store. I didn't mention it to anyone. I was starting to keep things bottled up. I was trying to hold it together, and just let the medical professionals guide me on this unknown path. But it seemed like even they weren't getting it right. Neither was I. No one was.

Day 34 — December 28, 2014

The following morning was the last Sunday of the year, and I needed to attend worship more this day than any. Growing up, my parents often spoke of God and the Word, so spirituality was very much a part of my rearing. Because my mother worked on the weekends, we only attended church occasionally. In high school, I started to attend church on my own and got involved in activities like the choir. As a teenager, church was more of a social outlet. Spirituality began to take on a much bigger role in my life as a young adult. After my mother passed away, my outlook on life and spirituality became foggy and derailed. It took a few years to find my way through this fog, but I eventually did. I began spending more time attending church and found my spirituality reinvigorated. The Temple Church had a great outreach program for youth, college students and the young adult demographic. The young-adult Bible study class had a tone and curriculum that was appealing to those who were familiar with current happenings. There was even a basketball ministry where members could play pickup games. I was involved in music and video in my personal life, so joining the audio-visual team was a natural choice. I found a lot of support and comradery which helped me grow in many ways.

This particular Sunday, I decided to let Brandy and Blake sleep in, since we all had a long week with the holiday. While I was driving to church, I noticed the pink tint remained in my eye, and I could see the top of the red glob in my vision without having to look down. Once I arrived at church, I went straight to the audio-visual room to get to work. I took my place in the audio/visual room.

I didn't say much to anyone, which wasn't like me at all. I just couldn't get myself out of a worried mindset, and I never wanted to give the impression that anything was wrong. I didn't want to believe there was.

Church was high in the spirit that morning. For many, the holidays are the hardest time of the year because they face going through them without the people they love. Some are in other places and some have passed on. Either way, it causes many emotions they would normally hide.

As the choir sang "Total Praise," my brother, Pastor Darrell A. Drumwright, stepped to the pulpit and addressed the presence of a strong spirit in the church. He called for those going through anything in their mind, body, or spirit to stretch their hands toward the altar.

"If you are struggling with anything during this time, I ask that you call out your sickness, emotion, or circumstance and give it to God. Ask him to remove that burden, in the name of Jesus," he stated to the congregation. I could see on the camera monitors crowds of people stretching their hands and calling out their burdens. Before I knew it, I had taken my hand off of the camera controller and stretched my hands toward the altar. I didn't know what was wrong with me, but I knew that I needed help dealing with it. Who better than God?

I left church feeling better than I had when I arrived, but not seeing any better than before. I couldn't tell if my vision was getting worse or if the tears I shed during the service were affecting my vision.

I drove home to visit with my dad and David, but neither of them was there. I sent them both a text saying I was hoping they would be home and that I just wanted to say "I Love You." I did that occasionally, so I knew it wouldn't startle them to see that text.

I got to Brandy's home and got back in the bed. She and Blake were up, but laying around and relaxing. After an emotional church service, I was tired and didn't want to think about my vision, so I took a nap. When I woke up, it was 6:30 p.m., which meant I had been asleep for about four hours. When I sat up, blood rushed in front of my vision. I got up quickly to check myself in the mirror, and the blood was now visible in about a third of my vision. However, it was never visible externally. Brandy called for me from the other room, but I couldn't break my silence. I walked into the spare bedroom where she was ironing clothes.

"Hey, baby! You were tired, weren't you?" I nodded my head, agreeing with her. As I nodded, the blood in my vision swooshed around like water on top of oil. Not sure what to say, I left the room and went back to the restroom, where I sat on the toilet. I didn't have to use the restroom, but I didn't want anyone to see me in a daze. What felt like minutes must have been much longer, because Brandy came in suggesting that I had been in the bathroom longer than normal.

"Hey, you okay? I was going to ask you to run out to get us dinner. I'll call it in and pay," she said while looking at her reflection in the mirror. In my mind, I answered her question, but in reality, I was stuck. She touched my face and pulled my head up so I could look at her. She saw the worry on my face and asked, "What's wrong baby? I know that look."

I tried my best not to shed any more tears, but I felt so helpless that they quietly begin to fall to the floor beneath me. She wiped my eyes and said, "I'll drop off Blake at my mom's house in the morning, and you and I will go to your doctor appointment together." The doctor's office opened at 7 a.m., and I aimed to be there when the doors opened. I was starting to believe that this was going to be the longest 13 hours of my life.

We ordered pizza and salad for dinner. Then, Brandy, Blake, Minx and I laid in the bed and watched TV, while I tried not to worry. Brandy and I knew what I was experiencing wasn't normal, not even for a diabetic. So, we were eager to get answers.

They fell asleep as I watched TV as best as I could. It seemed like every time I sat up there was more blood in my vision. I closed my eyes; temporarily not seeing anything at all was better than the red glob. I began talking to God.

Dear heavenly, Father. I come asking You to heal me, deliver me, and set me free.

Heal me.
Deliver me.
Set me free.
Amen.

After praying, I thought to myself, *I will get to the doctor and get seen tomorrow. Things will be okay. Things will be different.*
I just didn't know how different things would be.

Day 35 — December 29, 2014

I woke up early that morning feeling uneasy about everything. Why my vision continued to get worse was more than unsettling. It was becoming downright scary. I couldn't see anything in my right eye and vision in the left one became more and more hazy. The glare from direct light was becoming unbearable. The red blob of blood had become more visible since Saturday, and it seemed to grow by the hour. At least I was off of work and on break from school, so I didn't have to worry about trying to manage those responsibilities while my health was going downhill.

I'm good. I'll be good, I thought to myself.

I reached over to Brandy lying in bed next to me. She was sound asleep. At the moment I just let my mind relax. I smiled to myself and rolled over to find her face and give her a kiss. I thought it must have been quite early because it was still pitch black outside. I rubbed my eyes to clear my vision so I could find my way to the bathroom.

As I got out of the bed, I stepped on a pair of Brandy's shoes. She often left her shoes in the middle of the floor, and sometimes she even placed shoes on the steps. It was definitely not my favorite thing that she did, and it made me scratch my head. I remembered the first time I visited her home. Never had I seen so many shoes lined perfectly going up a flight of steps. And as many times as I had almost broken my ankle walking down these steps, I still loved her.

On this particular day, I looked down and didn't see any shoes on the floor. As a matter of fact, I couldn't see anything at all. I walked toward the wall where I knew the light switch was located, and I collided, shoulder first, into the bathroom doorway creating a loud thud. I backed up until I could feel the edge of the bed hit my calves. As I sat down, I began rubbing my eyes as if there was something in them. Nothing.

"God…God, no," I muttered under my breath, trying not to wake Brandy up. I closed my eyes and gathered myself. *Dude, just open your eyes and see your way to the bathroom. Okay?* I opened my eyes.

At this moment, my heart felt like it was in my throat. I was having a hard time swallowing and my breathing came in short, shallow gasps. Random thoughts started to come into my mind as I sat there trying to make sense of what was going on. I started to think about my late mother and how she would stay on me about my health. Then I thought of my family, fearing how I would have to tell them this. Then I thought of Brandy, who was lying right next to me. I was calm, but at the same time more frightened than I could ever remember in my life. I thought about how my eye doctor had been telling me that everything was going to be okay, and I knew something had gone completely wrong. Lost in thought, I felt Brandy move in the bed.

As she awakened, she softly asked, "Hey baby, you up?"

I reached my hand toward her and rested it on her back and replied, "I think... I mean... Yeah, I'm up." I sounded unsure and confused. I could tell she was half-sleep, but growing alert hearing the tremble in my voice.

"You okay?" she asked with concern.

At this moment, so many thoughts and emotions were running rampant in my head. Regret after regret began to fester in my mind.

Should I have taken more ownership of my health much sooner, and not just trusted that the doctors were right when they said 'everything will be okay'?

Maybe I should have proposed to Brandy sooner. Will she still want me now?

I should have started graduate school earlier. How would I be able to finish school if I couldn't see?

Had I procrastinated too long with my attention to my health, my career goals and my relationship dreams? Now I might not have time to accomplish all the plans I had for my life.

I felt like I was being locked in a dark room with no windows or doors to exit. The walls were closing in on me.

"Daniel?" she said, jolting me from my thoughts.

I exhaled and said, "I can't see."

She exclaimed, "No. You can't be serious!"

A tear fell from my eye. She pulled me close and cried. I prayed that it was a mistake and that I would open my eyes and see her face. I looked toward her. Nothing.

***

"I have the address in my GPS. I need to stop to get gas. Then, we will go straight there," Brandy said as she guided me to the passenger side of the car. She had already called her job to let them know she wouldn't be coming in, and she drove Blake and me to an emergency visit to Dr. K.'s office.

As I sat helplessly in the passenger side front seat, my mind was racing. I was thinking to myself:

What did I do to deserve this?

Life comes in waves; we have moments where we rise and moments when it all comes crashing down. Though I had felt that life had been unfair at times, I always knew I was blessed to have the love and support of the people I had in my life.

"All gassed up. Let's go," Brandy said getting back in the car.

I learned to meet intimidating moments head on and be confident. I knew that how we respond in those uncomfortable situations is what makes the biggest impression and impact on our lives. We grow and reveal more about ourselves through the challenges we face. The sense of accomplishment is so much more rewarding when completing a challenging task, getting past a daunting obstacle, or overcoming an insecurity. And the reward is also greater.

"In 1,000 feet, make a right onto Old Hickory Boulevard," the voice from the GPS stated. I felt the car turn right as I sunk deeper into my thoughts.

I felt as though the future I had been trying to build toward for years was being threatened in this moment. How was I supposed to take care of a family when I couldn't even take care of myself? My dreams as a young man of being an All-American football player and collegiate athlete had already been derailed. Now, I felt like I was being robbed of my dreams again. Would I ever be able to now become the husband, father, supportive friend to my Dunnies, or successful business person that I desired to be?

This car ride to the doctor was truly an epiphanic moment; I didn't know the previous weeks had all been leading up to this day when my sight would be completely gone.

"In 500 feet, take a left on to I-65 South," said the female voice from the GPS.

"We're not far," Brandy said as I continued reminiscing and Blake slept in the back seat. We didn't want to scare him with everything that was going on. So, we didn't tell him how much I was struggling with my sight.

"In .5 miles, take Exit 66," the GPS said. I felt Brandy merge into the far right-hand lane and exit a short time later.

"We are here," Brandy said as the car came to a stop. This had been the longest car ride of my life. As Brandy got out of the car to come on my side and help guide me in, I said a short prayer. This was not the way I hoped to prepare for the New Year, but I was here at the doctor's office, once again.

***

I often say that December 29, 2014, was the "first day of the rest of my life." The day began in complete darkness, and I was on a journey to find light. To find answers. To find some logical explanation for the mysterious condition that had literally blindsided me.

Unfortunately, after an emergency visit with Dr. K, I walked away with nothing more than another referral to another doctor – a retina specialist – and only a guess as to why the blood vessels in my eyes were leaking and not healing properly from my previous procedures. "Something is going on with your blood," Dr. K concluded.

At that point, it was time to inform my entire family of the severity of everything I had been trying to deal with. I didn't want to hide it any longer, and quite frankly, I *couldn't* hide it even if I wanted to.

Even though I had been having major problems with my eyes, I still never believed that I would be completely without sight. In my mind, it just wasn't possible.

I was exhausted. I didn't know what was coming next. But the one thing I did know, was that I couldn't take another step without my family's full support. Brandy agreed, and she helped me reach out to my brothers, my aunt, and my dad.

It was time to tell them that I was totally blind.

I couldn't fathom how they would react, especially my father. He didn't handle bad news well, especially when it came to his children. I decided to call my Aunt Maychelle, who was like a second mother to me. Brandy dialed the number and gave me the phone.

"Hey sugar! What you got going on?" she said when answering the phone.

"Hey, Aunt Maychelle. I need to let you know something," I replied. I took a deep breath and gave her the news. She let out a sound of disbelief and grief. I knew that delivering this update to my loved ones would be tough, so I asked my aunt to share the news with the rest of the family.

Brandy took the rest of the day off from work, and we spent time together to try to make sense of things. As calls started to come in, I spoke to relatives and friends.

"It's your dad, babe," Brandy stated with a bit of hesitation when my phone rang again. I took a deep breath and answered.

"Hey, Daddy."

Before he spoke, he cleared his throat, trying to collect himself. "Hey, hey there Daniel. What's going on?" It was clear that he had not gotten much information, which meant his anxiety level was through the roof. I calmly explained what was happening, and he began sobbing.

"Daniel, this is not making sense. Why can't they tell you why this happened? You know what? I'm gonna call a lawyer, because that doctor did this to you," he said as he added countless expletives. I knew the conversation would quickly go this route. I understood, though. Parents' first natural instinct is to protect their children and defend them against anyone they believe wronged them.

As we continued talking, I did my best to stay calm, and my dad began to relax. My ability to keep my composure under pressure was always a soothing point in our relationship.

"Daddy, I know you are angry, but we have to stay positive and level-headed during this time. I'm scared, so I need you to be positive for me. Brandy will drop me off at home in the morning, and we will talk more then."

He agreed, even though he was not totally satisfied with my response. As I ended the call, Brandy rubbed my thigh to comfort me.

"That conversation took a lot," I said to her.

Brandy looked at my phone and saw that my brother was calling. "It's Darrell," she said. Before I knew it, I was in tears. With a trembling voice, I said, "Hello."

"Hey, bud. How you feeling?" he asked. I couldn't find the words to respond, so I just cried.

"Awe, Daniel. I know you are scared, but I promise we will get through this," Darrell replied trying to contain his own emotions. Darrell always had a way of making me feel safe and secure. All I wanted was to see my big brother.

"Little bro, don't be down. Never forget that momma and our grandmother, Momma Rose, are always with us," Darrell reminded me. "Remember all the things they used to say?

'You might be down, but you're not out. You're still alive.'

'If the truth hurts, then fix it.'

'If you're here to experience this trial, then just figure it out and be ready to receive your blessing'

'Keep going even through tribulations. Don't let this moment define the rest of your life.'

I was still at a loss for words, so I just agreed, and we ended the conversation.

Quite a bit of time went by without any calls. I rested on Brandy's lap, as she softly stroked the side of my head. I laid there hoping to fall asleep and wake up from this nightmare. Just as my eyes began to get heavy, my phone rang. "It's David, baby," Brandy said. I immediately began to tear up, once again.

"Hey, Daniel. I just wanted to call and check on you. I got Brandy's text. Geez, I'm not sure what's up, but I'm..." He paused. Then, I heard him sniffling and I lost it.

"I'm so sorry, David. I'm sorry that you have to see and hear me like this," I whaled into the phone. I hated that everyone would have to see me this way, especially my baby brother. I had never felt more helpless and vulnerable in my life.

"Daniel, you have nothing to be sorry about. You have been the best big brother, other than Darrell because he's the actual best big brother," David said to lighten the mood. I laughed.

"You've always been there and had my back. It's just my turn, now."

"We're going to get through this together, okay? Me, you, Daddy, Darrell, Brandy, all our family and friends." He was firm and confident. We talked for 15 minutes until it was time for him to prepare for work. I cried even more after we ended our call, but not because I was sad. Instead, I was emotional and grateful for my baby brother's words of encouragement.

Day 42 — January 5, 2015

Ironically, my appointment with the retina specialist at Vanderbilt University Medical Center and my appointment at Tennessee Oncology were scheduled for the same day.

I spent the night before thinking about both appointments and creating scenarios on how the doctors would respond to my conditions. I imagined I'd leave each appointment with positive outlooks and swift recovery times.

Aunt Maychelle took me to my appointments. She carefully led me to the car, and we began our day heading to the first appointment. After fighting traffic, we arrived at Vanderbilt.

I quietly sat in the cold waiting room as I anticipated my visit with the doctor. Because I was in complete darkness, I attempted to absorb my surroundings and use all my other senses to "see" without eyes. I tried to figure out the ethnic backgrounds of the technicians who assisted me by listening to the tones and accents in their voices.

"Aunt Maychelle, the guy who helped me was black and the ladies were white, right?"

She laughed and replied, "No, baby. One was Latino and the other was Asian." Not long after that exchange with my aunt, a lady with a strong Arabic accent came through the doors. After listening to her speak for only a few short moments, I knew she was the doctor.

"Mr. Drumwright? Good morning. I looked at the scans and images of your retinas." She grabbed my hand from the armrest, as I couldn't see her reach out to me. "So, this all came on in the span of a few weeks?" she asked.

As I explained the course of events, I heard two male voices from across the room discussing my circumstances. The doctor exhaled before replying.

"Sir, your retinas are not in good condition at all. Your left eye has a lot of blood floating around. Your retinas are detached, and the amount of scarring you have in both eyes normally doesn't happen in such a short time, even in diabetics."

She explained that detached retinas meant that the thin layers of tissue at the back of my eyes had pulled away from their normal positions. The retinal cells had been separated from the blood vessels that supplied oxygen and nourishment to my eyes. I figured this explained my reduced vision and the specks I had seen floating in my eyes.

This was not the scenario that I had played out in my mind the night before. I slumped over and hung my head as she continued talking. I could hear my aunt ask several questions, but I couldn't process anything she said. I eventually heard the doctor respond.

"Ma'am, I cannot lie. It's possible he'll never see again," the doctor said to

Aunt Maychelle. "I can't promise anything, but we will do our best to help him. I suggest scheduling a surgery to address the structural issues with both of his eyes. Because he has diabetes, this was most likely caused by diabetic retinopathy, a complication with the eyes that sometimes occurs when your blood sugar is not controlled. The surgery will reveal if there's any chance to remove scarring and restore vision."

We set a date for surgery for the following week.

The rest of the appointment was a blur, and we couldn't leave there soon enough. We walked to Aunt Maychelle's car, got in and closed the doors. I grabbed her hand and stated, "I will not be blind for the rest of my life." She squeezed my hand and replied, "I know you won't."

I began thinking about everyone in my family and circle of friends who were waiting to hear a good report from my appointment. In fact, my phone had rung several times while we were in the office. I had missed calls from Brandy, my brothers and my supervisor. But the only hopeful thing the doctor said was, "we will do our best."

Before we pulled off, my aunt helped me dial the numbers on my cell phone and I gave brief updates to Brandy and my supervisor, Courtney. I was hopeful to have better news from my second appointment of the day.

***

As we pulled up to the hospital that housed Tennessee Oncology, my aunt asked, "Did Dr. Wolfe say what she was sending you to an oncologist for?"

"No, she didn't," I responded. I knew it was because she saw abnormalities in my blood work, but I didn't know any more than that. Maybe I didn't want to know.

After getting checked in and giving blood, we were placed in a waiting room. My aunt was quieter here than she was at the eye doctor.

"Baby, did Dr. Wolfe say that she saw anything in particular? I only ask because I'm very familiar with what oncologists look for." I could tell she was hinting at something.

I replied, "No. She just said that an elevated white blood cell count could mean several things, and she wants me to get checked out to make sure it's not anything serious."

I knew that she was concerned. Hell, I was very concerned. I began to feel like the imminent news from the doctor would not be positive. I thought back to the call from Dr. Wolfe's office while I was at work weeks ago, and how they communicated limited information over the phone. My anxiety was now at an all-time high.

The door to the waiting room finally opened, and I heard a male voice greet us. It was Dr. Erter. He began asking me about my health, and I told him the entire story that led us to him.

11 doctor visits with five different doctors
A laser procedure
A needle injection
And a lot of distress and discomfort.

After listening very attentively to my extended narration of my circumstances, he began to describe what he'd observed.

"I did find something when examining your blood under the microscope today," he said. "It's called chronic myeloid leukemia."

Leukemia.
Cancer.

I had just been diagnosed with cancer. I was at a loss for words, and I was instantly in a darker place than being blind had led me to. I had read about possible causes of an elevated white blood cell count. Never did I actually think it was leukemia. Other than low energy and my vision issues, I didn't feel sick.

"Many people find out they have leukemia by getting ill and it seems like they can never recover, or getting an injury that continues to linger, or getting a cut that just keeps bleeding," Dr. Erter continued. "In your case, it seemed to attack the blood vessels in your eyes. This could explain why the procedures you had did nothing to correct your vision. They likely made things worse. We will send your blood work off to the lab for complete confirmation, but I'm pretty certain that's what is going on."

The bigger picture was beginning to come into focus for me. My blood was not clotting properly because I had leukemia, so the incisions on my eyes from the procedures were not healing the way they should.

The oncologist explained how chronic myeloid leukemia affects the body, effectively turning blood into molasses, damaging blood vessels, and causing ailments such as neuropathy, severe weight loss, chronic fatigue, hemophilia, or vision issues.

To say that I was in shock would have been the understatement of my life.

Being blind was the "Oh shit" moment that knocked me on my ass.

A leukemia diagnosis was the "Aha" moment that kicked me while I was down.

Although I had not put much thought into it, there was a substantial history of cancer on both my mother's and father's side of the family. My mother, her oldest sister and my paternal grandmother all died from cancer. But I was still not prepared to receive a cancer diagnosis of my own. I began to cry, and although my aunt was just as devastated as I was, she was able to keep it together enough to ask the necessary questions.

"Daniel is scheduled to have surgery next week on his eyes. Should we hold off on that?"

"Could the surgery have negative results if we don't treat the leukemia first?"

These were all good questions, but I didn't want to wait a single day longer than necessary to see again. The idea of postponing the surgery was a non-starter for me.

"You should definitely wait," Dr. Erter responded. "We need to try and get his white blood cell count down. If he has this surgery beforehand, it is almost certain that it would be ineffective and possibly make things worse."

This made me angry.

"So, I might not only die, but I could die blind?! That's bullshit," I sarcastically interrupted. I was always the positive one in the midst of trials, but there was nothing positive about this moment. I wasn't about to pretend. I felt defeated.

"Daniel, don't think like that," my aunt said to me as she wiped tears from my face. "You have to believe that things will work. If you don't believe, why even try? I know you are hurting, and Lord only knows why you have to deal with this, but this is your cross. You can either carry it or you can quit before you even give yourself a chance."

She then turned her attention back to Dr. Erter.

"How do we treat this and how long does it take to see changes in his blood work?" my aunt asked him.

"Well, there are a few medications out there to treat this type of leukemia. The good thing is that the medications have a high success rate. Several people have had this form of leukemia for years, and they live normal lives. Daniel, we are going to start you on Tacigna, which is an oral chemotherapy. It's an aggressive medication so it has several side effects, but it's typically not as rough on your system as liquid chemotherapy."

As down as I was, that small bit of positive information gave me hope.

"Is there a chance that this medication doesn't work?" I asked.

The doctor exhaled and replied, "Well, there is always a chance that this won't work. If oral chemotherapy doesn't work, then there is a chance that nothing will. Let's not worry about that, though. Let's remain hopeful. We are going to see you back next week to check your blood counts. If they are going down, as I suspect they will, you can have the surgery as planned."

The doctor left the room to prepare my prescription and instructions. I heard my aunt make a phone call.

"Hey, baby. Yeah, I'm here with Daniel," she stated. I could hear the voice on the other end of the call quite clearly. It was her son – my cousin – Decosta.

"Just talk to him. He needs to hear you," she said to Decosta before passing me the phone. I wanted to say something, but at that moment I was paralyzed. As I tried to speak with tears pouring from my eyes, nothing came out.

"Dunny, I hear you. You don't have to say anything. I got you. I'm here with you, and I'm sorry." Decosta always found the right words to help me through tough spots. "Man, I hate this. Why you, again? I don't want to question God, but how? Life has been really unfair, but you just keep ticking. You got to overcome, again. You got this, though. We got this," he cried as he talked.

Somehow, I managed to utter a simple reply. "Yeah, I got it."

I gave my aunt the phone back. As she began to talk, she was interrupted by another call coming in. "I got to take this call. It's Darrell." She had texted him while the doctor was giving us the diagnosis. She eventually gave me the phone and I could hear him crying.

"Daniel, don't think for a second that we not gonna fight this." His voice was comforting, as it always was. I remember being in fifth grade and him calling home from college. I would eavesdrop from a landline phone on mute in another room as he talked to our mother. She would give me up by saying, "You know who is on the phone, too."

"Hey, Chub Scrubs!" as he affectionately called me when I was a little boy. I would laugh and chat with him about whatever was going on in an 11-year-old's life. But now, I was a grown man looking for comfort from my biggest role model.

"Darrell, I'm scared." That's all I could get out. Just as Decosta did, he reassured me that he would be there through everything. At that moment it was evident that I would be surrounded by family and friends who would be there with me. Their presence would be a Godsend.

Day 47 — January 10, 2015

As word got out about my illnesses, support started pouring in from all directions. I received texts, calls, and online messages from many friends and family showering me with love. Many of them offered to spend time with me to help pick up my spirits, or even help me run errands like taking me to the pharmacy to pick up my chemotherapy medicine. I had always had a large network of friends, family, and cohorts, and it was humbling to see how much they cared. Their comfort and support gave me even more confidence that I would recover and this would all be over soon.

I had to focus on staying calm and optimistic about my circumstances. When at home, I sat outside on the back patio for hours, thinking about life and everything I hoped to do once this nightmare was over. I turned my eyes toward the trees and lake, trying to see anything. I tried to see the nature and wildlife that I had grown so accustomed to admiring. I thought of the two little boys and little girl who lived next to us coming up and saying, "Hey Mr. Daniel." The images of what I could no longer see were more detailed in my memory than they ever seemed before.

Would I ever see Brandy's face again?

Would I be able witness the expression on her face when I presented the diamond engagement ring to her?

Would I completely lose my independence and the ability to move freely from place to place as I'd done all my adult life?

How would I make it back and forth to work?

Had I seen beautiful places such as the Las Vegas strip for the last time?

I knew night was approaching when the sun no longer warmed my skin. I hung my head and began praying, asking God for something that resembled a breakthrough. I asked him to show me that this wasn't the end of my story. I didn't know if my vision would be the same, or if I'd even get through the leukemia, but I needed a sign that He was listening.

Day 49 — January 12, 2015

After several days, I woke up one morning with what felt like an answer from God. I was awakened by light. This was exciting and shocking at the same time because I had not been able to see light for days. I could discern the colors of the objects near me, but everything looked like mush because nothing had detail or shape. I was only experiencing this light reception in my left eye.

I felt my way upstairs to my father's room and told him the news. He was thrilled.

"Can you see what this says?" he asked me. I assumed he was holding something up. Maybe a container.

"Daddy, I can't see that," I answered. "I see the color, but not detail."

He grabbed my hand and replied, "But you definitely can see more than darkness, right?" I nodded my head, and he squeezed my hand. I could tell that lifted his spirits. It did a lot for mine, too! My dad informed my aunt, and we called Brandy together to share the news. They all were overjoyed.

My coworker suggested that I try to get an appointment at Tennessee Retina. Her mother had retina surgery there, and they were very pleased with the treatment they received. Because I still hadn't found a doctor that I felt truly connected to, I was hopeful that maybe I'd find someone that was more empathetic, and whose bedside manner put me more at ease. Tennessee Retina was able to squeeze me in that day, so I headed to Centennial Medical Center to be seen.

I spent the first hour going from room to room, taking scans and images of my eyes. The staff asked me on several occasions, "Are you okay? Are you in any discomfort?" I was so high on hope that I answered positively and graciously.

Once again, I began playing out the scenarios in my head. I envisioned the doctor giving me positive feedback, and I imagined myself happy to have found a new doctor to help me. I was confident that we would leave feeling even better than when we came.

"Mr. Drumwright, I've reviewed the images, and I'd like to take a look at your eyes myself with the instruments that I have here," said Dr. Schneider, one of the physicians at Tennessee Retina. As I leaned into position, the doctor sat behind a scope to examine my retinas and see what was there.

I gave Dr. Schneider a full summary of events that had occurred with my eyes. He began saying medical terms that I couldn't understand, and I could hear the technician typing notes as the doctor spoke. I could see the light as Dr. Schneider looked in my left eye.

"Mr. Drumwright, I have never seen such a buildup of scarring in anyone's eye," he commented.

With a hint of disappointment, I replied, "I've not been able to see anything for weeks. That was until this morning. I can see light, now."

I hoped by telling the doctor there had been some changes, he would have a more optimistic outlook than before. This was not the case. He began stating that the condition of my retinas was grave, and they would need to perform a vitrectomy, a delicate procedure that requires using high-tech surgical equipment to remove scar tissue from my retinas to try to restore any vision. While he was aware of my leukemia diagnosis, he felt that diabetes was the most likely culprit for my sight problems. Nevertheless, he concurred with the previous assessment from the oncologist that surgery should only happen if my white blood cell counts returned to an acceptable range.

"We want to start with your right eye, as this looks to be the one that has the most promise," the doctor explained.

Before he could get out another word, I interrupted him saying, "My right eye? Why would you start there?!?! That doesn't make sense! I just told you I can see something in my left eye. And this is the eye I last had sight in!"

The room grew quiet as I ended my verbal barrage. The young doctor placed his hand on my shoulder and said confidently, "I can't imagine how you are feeling at this moment, but as your doctor, I see things differently. I can see the structural damage, and I believe it will be more beneficial to start on your right. When it heals up enough, which should take three to four weeks, we will work on the other eye. I can't promise that you will see again out of either eye. But I promise to do my very best."

By this time, I was quietly in tears. Though there was a room full of people, I felt like I was alone. I felt the hand of my aunt grab me and say, "Daniel, I need you to trust that he is doing what he believes is right. Even if you don't believe it, he is going to do his best for you."

I didn't like what Dr. Schneider was saying, but I believed he cared about helping me. He felt genuine and seemed knowledgeable.

Before leaving, we set a conditional surgery date, as we still had to wait until I was cleared by the oncologist. If my white blood cell count didn't improve, then we wouldn't be able to move forward with surgery anyway.

I went to Tennessee Retina thinking that a new doctor might see things differently and offer a new perspective on my condition. However, he came to the same conclusion that the retina specialist at Vanderbilt did.

I needed surgery.

I found myself disappointed once again. My aunt and I sat quietly in the car as she drove me home. I imagined waking up and finding myself back in Las Vegas. The city lights flashed against my skin and my silhouette outlined the strip with each step I took. Before I knew it, we were at my condo, and my aunt was helping me to the door. She reminded me to stay positive and patient.

"Once we get your blood straight, we can get them eyes together. God works in ways that man can't. Just hold tight, okay?" I didn't have much to say, so

I agreed and walked inside my condo, where she got me settled in. David and my dad were at work, so she wanted to make sure I had everything I needed before she departed. Not long after she left, I received a call from Brandy. I informed her of what happened at the appointment and how disappointed I was.

"Daniel, I work in health care. I know how doctors can be. He won't tell you something that he isn't sure of. The doctor can only do his part. You have to be faithful and hopeful. Your vision may never be as good as it was before, but I believe that it will be good enough for you to live a long and meaningful life. This is a test," Brandy said.

"What if I never get any sight back?" I asked her. "What if I'm blind forever?"

"You could be completely blind, and I'd love you the same." I sensed her smile through the phone.

Day 52 — January 15, 2015

The end of the week finally came and I was eager to get to the oncologist to give my blood sample. Aunt Maychelle picked me up from home that morning, and we stopped at the McDonald's drive through to get a chicken, egg, and cheese biscuit – one of my favorite breakfast sandwiches. We finished our food in the parking lot of the medical facility and headed inside.

Our wait was brief, as they called us in shortly after arriving and signing in. I was escorted to the nurse's station where the nurse wrapped a super-sized rubber band around my arm, got a blood sample, and walked my aunt and me to an empty room where we waited for the doctor.

"How do you feel, baby?" my aunt asked.

"As much as I've gone through lately, I feel okay. I don't feel bad," I replied. "The Tacigna hasn't made me feel any worse. I'm just hoping for good news." As we continued to talk, the doctor entered the room.

"So, I'm gonna cut to the chase," the doctor said as I anxiously sat in the chair. "Your white blood cell count is down to 39,000. It is still elevated above normal levels, but you've only taken the medicine for a short time. So, you are right on schedule."

I was so relieved. But, before getting too excited, I asked, "So can I have the surgery to repair the damage on my retinas? It's scheduled for Tuesday."

He replied, "I don't see any reason to postpone it any longer. I will let your surgeon know you are good to go."

We made a follow up appointment for one month and we left. We called everyone we knew and shared the news that I was cleared for surgery on my right eye. We were all excited.

Day 55 — January 18, 2015

On Sunday, we went to church. Naturally, word had gotten around about my conditions. We were met at the door by several concerned church members who loved on us from the minute we got inside. During the worship service, my brother extended an invitation to come forward for the altar call. This was a sacred time when parishioners were offered the opportunity to go to the front of the sanctuary for prayer. The number of attendees who responded to the call varied; it could be anywhere from a handful of people to half of the congregation. This was a day that I responded to the call.

During the altar call, I made my way down front with Decosta on my right side and Brandy on my left. This was the beginning of me learning how to use and trust all of my senses to fully function. I placed my hand on Decosta's shoulder and I took Brandy's hand, the way a man naturally takes hold of his woman; they were my guides. I inconspicuously followed the lead from their subtle body movements; when they shifted their weight in a certain direction, I seamlessly glided with them. I imagine it would have been nearly impossible for an outside observer to tell that I was blind and my loved ones were serving as my eyes.

When we reached the altar, we stood with the others who responded to the call. We bowed our heads as Darrell prayed. Decosta and Brandy squeezed my hands during the prayer and I became emotional. This was a sobering moment before God, my brother, Decosta, Brandy and the entire congregation. This was the moment that it all became real. I always had a fear of appearing weak, and this was one of the weakest times of my life.

While I anxiously anticipated good results from the surgery that I was scheduled to undergo the next day, I was also intimidated by what *could* take place. All of the possible outcomes overwhelmed me. I was afraid that I might never see again. Even if my sight was restored, would I still be the same man that I was before all this happened?

Regardless of the outcome, I knew that God was preparing me to go through a journey, and I knew it was going to be a long one.

Day 56 — January 19, 2015

"Alright, we have all that insurance requirements and paperwork out of the way. I'm going to put this wristband on you, and we will get you prepped for surgery," said the lady at the registration counter. We were at Centennial Medical Center, and I was about to undergo the first surgery that I ever had on my eyes. The vitrectomy on my retinas was scheduled to last about three to four hours.

It was the anniversary of the passing of my mom. I wondered how she would have reacted to my condition. I missed her so much and felt the effects of her absence more this day than I could remember before. Thankfully, I had my aunts to help me through. My Aunt Maychelle guided my hand to the last line I had to sign before getting my wristband secured. She and I were then led to the elevator and sat in the waiting area, where my Aunt Brenda was waiting.

"Hey Daniel! How are you feeling?" my Aunt Brenda kissed and greeted me. "I'm okay. Just ready to get this done," I responded while playing with the tightly secured wristband. I was slightly nervous, but that was trumped by my hunger, as I was not allowed to eat before surgery. I had, also, thrown up the night before. I wasn't sure if it was the chemo or my nerves. I was cautiously hopeful that I would have significant post-surgery improvements, even though Dr. Schneider had his concerns.

I couldn't see, but I could tell there were several people in the waiting area. I would have plenty of time to think – and starve – so I tried to focus my thoughts on how it would be to see after going through all of this.

"Mr. Drumwright?" a woman's voice called out to me. My aunts and I made our way to the check-in desk, and then we followed the lady to another room to get my IV and vitals. She had a raspy voice and I imagined how she might look based on how she sounded.

An early 50s, slim lady who smokes.

As she asked me a number of screening questions, I began to grow more nervous. As we finished up with the nurse, we were led toward a room with a bed and television. I changed into the gown and lay in the bed. Another nurse came in and checked my blood sugar, blood pressure, temperature, and gave me anti-bacterial eye drops for the procedure. Then, the anesthesiologist entered the room.

"What's going on? How are we feeling today?" He gave me a rundown of how we would proceed.

"So, once they give me the 'all clear,' we will get you rolled back and ready to rock. That sound good?"

As he finished up, I had another 30 minutes before I headed to surgery. I tried to relax, but I couldn't. For the first time, I thought about the possibility of the surgery being ineffective. I wondered how life would be if I were totally blind. The fear of permanently losing my sight and losing my independence was overwhelming. I grew emotional and bitter, and I began to express the doubt that had creeped into my mind.

Both of my aunts consoled me and gave me encouragement to combat those thoughts. Then, I heard another familiar voice in the room.

"Hey, bud." It was my big brother, Darrell. He made his way across the room, and led all of us in prayer before the nurse took me to surgery.

As I was rolled back, I talked to God in my thoughts.

I'm not sure how this is going to end up. I have high expectations, but maybe I'm being unrealistic. I don't know what to expect, but I'm asking for a miracle. I'm asking to have my sight fully restored, but if I have to settle for lesser results, then please just let it be something I can live with. Allow me to be able to be independent. I will take just being able to see enough to take the bus. Please.

I was interrupted by Dr. Schneider.

"Hey there, Mr. Drumwright. We are going to go ahead and get you good and relaxed so that we can get the surgery started."

God, just get me through this, I thought quietly to myself.

I tried to focus on the brightness of the florescent ceiling lights. I listened to the nurse and doctor speak medical jargon and chat about randomness. I closed my eyes trying to ready myself for things to begin.

The next time I opened my eyes, the surgery was completed, and I immediately felt restrained.

"Mr. Drumwright, we're in recovery. You did well," a nurse said to me. Disoriented, I felt my face and discovered the amount of tape over the right side of my face. I imagined that I looked like The Phantom of the Opera.

"Can I go home? I want to go," I said as I had the worst headache and requested pain medication.

"Not yet. We have to get your blood sugar back regulated," a nurse said as I tried to figure out where she was located. I requested for Brandy to come into the recovery room, and tried to gather myself.

After nearly two hours in recovery, my blood sugar leveled out enough to allow me to be discharged. I was guided back to my hospital room where my aunts and brother waited for me. They helped me change out of the hospital gown and into my clothes, and we gathered my belongings. I was eventually rolled in a wheelchair to the exit door where Brandy awaited to take me to my Aunt Maychelle's home, where I would spend my next few weeks recovering.

"Don't forget to keep that head down to prevent your eye pressure from elevating," the nurse reminded me before loading me into the front seat. I strapped on my seat belt and laid the seat back to lie on my left side before we pulled off.

"Boy, you had the nurses ready to put you out of recovery," Brandy said as we pulled off. I was confused by her statement. I apparently caused more of a ruckus than I realized.

"You were demanding food and pain killers. I told them that you are normally mild-mannered and on your best behavior." Brandy was being light-hearted before easing into more substantive questions.

"So, how do you feel?" she asked.

I paused before I spoke.

"Hungry. I am hungry as hell! Please stop at Sonic," I said as nicely as I could. Brandy chuckled. I'm not sure whether I was moody from the anesthesia or just annoyed by the circumstances. But we got our food and made our way to my Aunt Maychelle and Uncle Gene's home.

When we arrived at their home, we were guided to the area in the living room that my aunt and uncle set up for me. They wanted me to have the best equipment and care possible, so they rented a chair designed to allow me to lay comfortably with my head in the downward position. I was instructed to lay face down for two weeks after the eye surgery to prevent the retina from detaching again. I wasn't looking forward to it, but I had no choice.

"How does this feel?" my aunt asked as she helped me get comfortable. "It's pretty much a massage chair. The opening will allow you to feed yourself without having to lift your head." It was better than I imagined it would be.

While Brandy and my aunt discussed plans to get me back and forth to appointments, my Uncle Gene arrived home and came to sit with me. My aunt and uncle played a big part of my upbringing. Their home had always been my second home growing up. Their son, Decosta, and daughter, Mia, were like brother and sister to me. Growing up, Decosta and I were together more often than not. Uncle Gene coached us in baseball, and it's easy to say that he was like a second father to me. He was just as devastated as anyone to get the news of my illnesses. To see how he was willing to step in and help in any way he could was a true blessing.

"How you feeling, biggun?" Uncle Gene asked. The truth was, my head was pounding, and I was feeling nauseous. I'm sure he could tell without me saying a word, so he just proceeded to help me get comfortable on the couch as he sat beside me.

"It's hard to see you going through all this, but you don't have to worry about the treatments or how you are going to take care of things," my uncle said. "Your aunt and I have been blessed and you know we are gonna make this process as smooth as possible. I just need you to hold on to faith. We don't know the road you have ahead, but we are walking it with you." He fed into me to have high hopes, but not be defeated if the results were not as I expected.

"All you need is 20/400 vision, and they can correct that with glasses. I'm praying for that."

I knew that 20/400 visual acuity falls in the severe vision loss category. But it was encouraging to hear that corrective measures existed that could help people achieve some normalcy and complete everyday tasks without too many special tools.

I went to bed that night wishing for a miraculous outcome at the follow-up appointment the next morning. The tape on the right side of my face bothered my skin. My cheek badly itched, and there was nothing I could do about it. My brother, David, stayed overnight at my aunt and uncle's home to keep me company and help out where he could. He asked if there was anything he could do to help, but there wasn't. I got as comfortable as I could and finally went to sleep.

Day 57 — January 20, 2015

The next morning at Tennessee Retina, a technician began removing my bandages in preparation to be examined by Dr. Schneider. She began using a wet paper towel and sterilized water to loosen up the tape and wipe the adhesive from my face. As the tape began to come free, I saw light. I was initially excited, but that quickly faded when my right eye became completely exposed. My peripherals were mute and my central vision was impeded by a dark mass. The areas of light I saw showed no image. It was as if I were looking through burnt plastic with a charred center. I tried to hide my emotions, but tears built up in my eyes. My body language said it all. I was devastated.

"Can you see this?" the nurse asked as a light passed in front of my eyes. I said nothing. I just nodded my head. The tech continued with a litany of tests. I reluctantly complied, hoping that it would be over quickly. Soon after she finished, Dr. Schneider came in to conduct his assessment.

"Everything is holding together. You had a lot of scar tissue, but we got as much as possible," he said after finishing his examination of my eye.

"So, is there more scar tissue you will remove in the future? And how long before we can do surgery on my left eye? That's the one I could see out of last. That one is going to be my saving grace," I said as the doctor read off notes to the technician in the room.

"Potentially," he said. "We have to see how things heal before we go back in. You are young, so I'm confident you will heal better than most. We can do your left eye in three weeks, as long as there are no problems with your right eye. How is your vision?"

"It's like the continent of Africa in the center of my vision. I can see light and some movement in a few areas, but nothing more," I said, hoping that he would confirm my symptoms with what he saw.

"Really? Let me look, again," he said. I was not elated by his sense of confusion as he looked at my retina.

"Yeah, everything looks intact, so just follow your orders. Lie face down or on your side to keep the pressure down, and we will see you in two weeks." The room grew silent as I waited for more information from Dr. Schneider.

"Is that it?" I asked as we were dismissed from the appointment. I couldn't believe that the results of the surgery were so minimal. Maybe it was too ambitious to expect overnight results. As if 24 hours could magically erase the damage to my eyes and the fear in my spirit that I'd experienced since early fall of the previous year. No, I wouldn't be returning to work on Monday morning, or meeting my Dunnies for drinks on Saturday. I wouldn't be driving, playing basketball, or taking trips to tourist attractions any time soon.

However, I knew what my goal was, and I shared my thoughts with my aunt as we got in the car to head home.

"I don't care what he says. My left eye is the better eye and once we get to it, I know I will see again."

Day 59 — January 22, 2015

I was really missing my mom, so I asked my brother, David, to take me to the cemetery to visit her grave. When we arrived there, he walked me to her grave and I sat next to her. It was the first time in three years that I went to visit for the anniversary of her death.

It had been 12 years since she passed, but it felt like I was just with her. A few months before I graduated high school, my mom lost her battle with breast cancer. She never disclosed that she had been dealing with cancer and chose not to treat it. We only found out because her pain became so unbearable that she had no choice but to go to the hospital. We were just finding out about her condition, but she had known for years. I would learn years later that my mother first knew about her condition as early as 1993. She had outlived any reasonable timeline known for a diagnosis such as hers, but the cancer had spread and her illness became harder to conceal. After an emergency room visit, she agreed to treat the cancer, but her body couldn't handle the radiation and chemotherapy. She didn't make it a month. I felt guilty for not seeing how much pain my mom was in. I beat myself up for not being able to help her when I felt she needed me the most.

I remember the night my mother passed very vividly.

We sat in the hospital room comforting her as her organs began to fail. A loud noise came from one of the machines hooked up to her. Doctors rushed into the room to take her to the intensive care unit. I was holding her hand as the staff began to rush her out of the room. I didn't want to let go, but I couldn't hold her hand and get through the opening of the door. As I let go, the staff continued to push her to the elevator. Before I knew it, she was in the elevator, but facing me. I looked her into her eyes, as she smiled at me one last time. And then, the elevator door closed.

In a rare occurrence, Nashville was hit by a snowstorm mid-January in 2003. There was no sign of the sun for several days. As we looked out of the window the morning of January 19, the sun finally peeked back from behind the clouds. As much of my family gathered to mourn my mother's passing, the sun shined back at us. It was like God's comfort, confirming that life goes on. Visiting her grave was one of the few things I could do to feel close to her again.

"Momma, I miss you so much right now. I know you are with me, but I wish I could hear your voice. I always found hope when you rooted for me. You were my biggest cheerleader, and I could really use those cheers right now. I will just have to do my best, like you always expected. You worked too hard, and I know that I would disappoint you if I didn't do my best to overcome this. I will try. Promise."

Before we left, I had David take me to my Grandmother Rose's grave, which was 15 feet away. I knew they would expect me to fight this and follow the orders I was given, so that was my goal.

When I lost my mom, I lost my biggest supporter. It left a void that was impossible for anyone to fill. Not even my father, who I deeply appreciated, could replace her love. My world was turned upside down, and it was during this time period that it seemed like all my plans started to become deferred.

At a time like this, I felt I needed my mother more than ever. But I gathered every ounce of strength within me to navigate this new life challenge that felt like it had the power to break me. I summoned the strength of those around me, and leaned on them more than I ever had in my life.

Day 72 — February 4, 2015

Despite my best efforts to precisely follow my doctor's orders – administering my prescribed eye drops, eating well-balanced meals to keep my blood sugar regulated, and staying face down for 90 percent of the day – I received heartbreaking news at my two-week follow-up appointment with Dr. Schneider.

"The scar tissue on your right eye has caused traction on your retina."

"The retina is detached, again."

"We need to work on your right eye, again."

I knew this meant that surgery on my left eye would be postponed. Frustration and angst consumed me.

I had imagined having an amazing recovery and testimony. Instead, it was starting to feel like I was living in the Twilight Zone, going through the redundant process of doctor's appointments, surgeries, and disappointment.

I'm blind. How was that even possible? How did I get here? I thought.

It was becoming harder and harder to remain hopeful and motivated to stay positive. Dejected by my circumstances, I retreated to a posture of sulking. All I wanted to do was sleep. My appetite was nonexistent. Not to mention, the Tacigna that was treating my high white blood cell count was beginning to make me feel ill. I took the chemo pill by mouth around the same time every morning and my stomach would be in knots within hours. Many times, I could barely keep food down. I'd wake up with headaches and body aches, which I never experienced before being prescribed the Tacigna. The medication also caused my skin to crack and peel. At times it felt like I had fire ants biting my skin.

I spent a lot of time replaying moments of my life in my head: great moments and those I wish I could forget. I wondered if my past created a path toward my present. Was this a punishment for something I did? And if so, what? I knew that God didn't work this way, but I couldn't help but question Him.

It was important for me to find inspiration again. I thought a lot about the life I had left on pause – my job, my friends, and most importantly, Brandy and Blake. I missed them all terribly. But not having the ability to get to Brandy and Blake on my own terms began to weigh on me. I had spent the past weeks away from them and the process was far from over.

So, we developed a schedule that allowed me to split my time at both places. Brandy dropped me off at my aunt and uncle's home on her way to work. On other days, I spent the night with her.

Being with Brandy made me feel like the man I always felt I was. We didn't spend a lot of time discussing my illnesses and in pity. Instead, we did our best to continue on with "normal" activities. We talked about the future, we went out to eat, and I listened to the television shows that they watched. As my senses became much stronger, we played a modified version of fetch; they took turns throwing coins across the room while I used my ears to locate them. It wasn't the life I had imagined, but it was a blessing to have them by my side.

Day 78 — February 10, 2015

After my second retina surgery in less than a month, I returned to my aunt and uncle's home where they had prepared the living room for me once again. After struggling to get comfortable for the evening, I eventually fell asleep, but woke up in the middle of the night having to use the restroom. I wasn't sure what time it was, but I knew that my aunt and uncle were asleep. I refused to wake them up so I could go relieve myself, so I got on my hands and knees to keep my face down, and crawled in the direction that I believed the bathroom was in. With a little effort, I was able to find it and relieve myself. As I exited and began to crawl back to my sleeping area, I heard my aunt.

"Seeing you crawl on the floor like that…," she said with emotion in her voice. Startled and a bit embarrassed, I stopped in my tracks. I felt her hand under my arm to help guide me the rest of the way.

"You're still the same person you have always been. You never want to ask for help. I know you wish you could get back to life the way it was. Trust that God will allow you to do just that. Stay determined, Daniel, but know that it's okay to need help."

My aunt got my uncle up to show me how to find my way to the bathroom in the future and implored me not to let my pride get in my way. We eventually made it back to the couch where she tucked me in. It was the first time I had been tucked in since a few months before my mom passed. After my final high school football game, I was completely drained. I fell asleep on the couch in our den. I remember waking up to my mom covering me with the comforter from our upstairs closet. That memory brought back emotions that I had long held on to. I hadn't missed Momma that much in a long time.

To help me cope with my anxiety, I began stretching and doing light workouts in the living room of my aunt and uncle's home. I continued listening to music, audiobooks my uncle got me, and sports TV to occupy my time. Occasionally, Mia logged onto my Facebook page and read posts and messages from my friends.

"We can definitely say that you don't lack support!" she said. It was true. I had so many individuals reach out to me and send well wishes that I was very humbled, indeed.

Day 102 — March 6, 2015

As the seasons began to change and the weather warmed early in Nashville, my spirit began to grow cold. I began to hear birds chirping in the morning. People began walking outside, soaking in the warm sun and nice weather. It angered me that I wasn't able to indulge in these pleasantries. My attitude began to change. I was short-tempered and sometimes irritable. I didn't want to come off as unappreciative or rude, so I often stayed to myself. I told myself that I just needed to get to mid-March and the greatly anticipated procedure on my left eye. That would determine everything.

Brandy, her mother Rhonda, and I had dinner at Olive Garden that Friday. The new trainee was having a difficult time keeping up with the pace. He apparently tried to hand me my drink.

"Oh, he's seeing impaired," Brandy stated to the young man. He apologized, seeming a little embarrassed. I was surely more embarrassed than he was. During dinner, Brandy and I discussed her upcoming birthday, which was in a few weeks.

"I had hoped to have had the surgery by then, but it doesn't look like that's going to happen. Really, I needed to wait so that I'm not down during your birthday," I said while having a sip of my soda. Brandy leaned in close and grabbed my right hand. Her fingers gently brushed against my skin.

"So, Daniel, tell me how you are feeling. I don't want to pry, but I just want to be sure you're okay."

Though I had my head facing forward, I could feel her looking at me from my right side. As I turned to face her, I imagined her smile and felt her eyes peering into me. Though I was elated to be with her, I was heartbroken not being able to see her face. I wanted to be truthful, but I didn't know how to without being coarse. My emotions had recently become unpredictable; one moment I was hopeful and positive, and the next I was disappointed, angry, and anxious. Before I could get anything out, she placed her hand under my chin to lift my head up.

"You are so strong, Daniel. You are such a good person. I am humbled to see all of the support you have received and how you have responded to this. It goes to show what type of man you have been. I don't know how you do it."

Neither did I. While she was still holding my chin, I pulled her towards me, and I reached out for her face. I kissed her on the cheek.

"Baby, I can't wait to see your beautiful face again," I said to her, and then we continued our evening.

We finished our meal and left for home. Blake stayed with Brandy's mother, so we had the house to ourselves. Brandy took me by the hand and guided me to the bedroom. I held her close and slowly placed her in the bed.

As we began to embrace each other, we quickly realized Minx was in the bed. We knocked her around until she had enough and hopped out. I may had been limited in my physical activity in the past two months, but I made up for it that night.

As we lay in the bed, I wrapped my arms around her, with my head face down. I didn't have to keep my head lowered all day, but I had to sleep face down or to the side to keep the pressure stable. As I caressed her arm, she told me that she wanted me there every weekend.

"I miss you being here. I thought about this, so you tell me how you feel. You can stay with your family Monday night through Thursday night. I can pick you up on Fridays, and you can stay until Monday. I can take you to your home or whatever you want to do on Mondays when I head to work. I just miss you when you're not here with me. Is that okay with you?"

Her reinforcement meant the world to me. Of course, I wanted to be with her, but I didn't want to inconvenience her. Because I lived close, and she worked five minutes from where my aunt and uncle lived, she was more than willing to drop me off and pick me up if it meant us getting to spend more time together. So, that became our new routine.

The loss of my sight threw a monkey wrench in my plans. I thought I would have already orchestrated the ultimate proposal with the engagement ring I had purchased in November. Instead, the princess-cut diamond ring lay stashed in the closet still waiting for the right time.

Day 107 — March 11, 2015

Today was the day I had been waiting weeks for. It was the appointment with Dr. Schneider to learn if I could move forward with surgery on my left eye. I wasn't in the mood to debate it. If we were in a position to do surgery, then that's what we were doing. I had been patient and obedient to the doctors' orders, and it was time to take control over my health. My aunt tried to convince me that the doctor would know best, but at this point I was making the executive decision.

"Mr. Drumwright, I'm happy to say that everything is holding together well. I know your vision hasn't improved, but maybe over time some of that scar tissue will start to settle and we will start to see progress. Then, we can go back in and remove more scar tissue to see if we get any more sight to return."

He paused for a moment, making comments under his breath.

"With that, I would like to monitor things for another week or so," he said before I quickly interrupted him.

"Hell no! You told me that if we got to this point and everything was stable that we could schedule surgery on my left eye. Has anything changed?"

I startled everyone in the room with my response. The doctor cleared his voice before replying.

"No, nothing has changed, but I don't think we need to rush into surgery on this eye. I know you're saying you have light reception in that eye, but from the scans there is more scar tissue on your retina than I've ever seen. That scar tissue is pulling at your retina and has lifted it from the back of your eye. I'm afraid that we will start pulling scar tissue off and it will damage the retina even more. It honestly may not be worth attempting surgery."

He hadn't said any of this before, which angered me immensely. I didn't care what he said. I knew how I felt and that was all that mattered.

"Is there any reason other than the ones that you just gave me that we can't move forward with the surgery on my left eye?" I asked him with a firm and direct tone.

"Circumstantially, no," my doctor said in a matter-of-fact tone.

I sat back and tried to fix my eyes toward him and replied, "Well, you're going to have a hard time getting rid of me today unless we schedule this procedure."

My doctor no longer resisted, and we began scheduling the surgery for my left eye. He ran through much of the same information he had before, but this time he gave me some additional information about my condition.

"I just want you to know that the scar tissue peeling is going to be a tedious process. I'm not sure how much damage is already done to your retina, but from what I can see, there is a lot of scar tissue to remove. All of this traction on your retina has created rips that will have to be welded with a laser. There's a chance that you will suffer significant vision loss from this surgery and a 35 to 40 percent chance that you will go completely blind in this eye. With the current condition of your right eye, it's possible you could be totally blind when this is all said and done. I just have to give you the facts."

Day 109 — March 13, 2015

Surgery on my left eye was planned for March 18, 2015, the day after Brandy's birthday. I didn't think about all of the information that my doctor gave me. I was just excited to be moving forward. We celebrated Brandy's birthday and my upcoming surgery at Morton's Steakhouse. We dressed in business formal attire and enjoyed a nice evening embracing the moment and looking forward to the future. For her birthday, I bought dinner, purchased a bouquet of roses that was delivered to her at work, and paid for a 60-minute full body massage at one of Nashville's premier massage studios.

"Baby, thank you so much for this! I can't wait for this massage," she said as we finished our meal.

I replied to her in my creeper voice, "But the massage you're getting tonight?! Oh, my goodness!" We both laughed hysterically. Being blind was devastating, but being around my friends, family, and Brandy made the time more bearable. That good energy definitely helped me keep my head above water.

As time for surgery grew closer, my focus fell more on the words that my doctor said during scheduling. I had so much hope for my left eye, but to hear him say that there was a significant chance that the procedure could leave me completely blind forever was frightening. It unnerved me to the point that I could not fall asleep at night. With only a few days before the surgery, all I could do was pray about it. I prayed before bed. I prayed before eating. I prayed before taking my medications. I even prayed before taking a shower.

Day 111 — March 15, 2015

That Sunday, we attended morning church service. I had questioned God, but I wasn't dumb enough to discount His power. After service, my younger brother met us at Brandy's house. I wanted to go home to visit with our neighbors and grab a few things, so he took me to do so. My neighbors, Joe, Karen, and Machel, were home and elated to see me. They had not had a chance to visit with me since everything occurred, so David guided me outside so that I could speak with them and my dad's girlfriend.

"I didn't know what to expect, but you look well, Daniel! I'm just happy that things are heading in the right direction and the leukemia is under control," Machel stated. I agreed, especially since I would be having my anticipated surgery in just a few days. We chatted about how everything happened and what led up to this moment.

"Wow, Daniel. I don't even know what I would do. So, you were in complete darkness, but now you can make out colors and shapes?" my dad's girlfriend asked as we gathered.

I replied, "I can make out most colors, but I cannot make out shapes. Everything is a big smudge. And this is with only my left eye. I can't see much of anything right now in my right."

I continued to explain what and how I saw.

"So, for instance, I can tell you all are right here since you are very close, but I can't tell who you are. I can kind of tell that there is some logo or embroidery on David's shirt," I paused as I touched David's shirt. His chest felt very soft as I rubbed my hands over the words.

"Daniel, that's Karen," my dad's girlfriend said to me as I still had my hand on her chest. If I wasn't red in the face from talking, I was surely now with embarrassment. "Well, now you know I'm not lying," I replied. Everyone got a good laugh, including me.

Day 114 — March 18, 2015

The morning of surgery, Brandy and I dropped Blake off with his grandmother before heading to the hospital. Upon arrival, I grabbed Brandy's hand and said a quick prayer before we got out of the car. Once I finished, she leaned in and kissed me.

"Let's get you put back together, Humpty Dumpty," she joked.

I replied in my creeper voice, "Oh my goodness! Don't tell them my nickname. Humpty!"

We met up with my aunts Maychelle and Sharon inside the hospital where we followed the steps of registering and getting ready for surgery. Sharon was my mom's spontaneous and slightly wilder sister. She traveled the world as a flight attendant and had been to more places than anyone I know. I was blessed to have another nurturing female in my life who did whatever she could to help.

I spoke silently with God again, telling Him I wouldn't have lofty expectations, but I at least needed a glimmer of progress to keep my faith and spirits intact. I prayed all the way back into the operating room. As I ended my prayer and opened my eyes, I could make out the distorted light from the halogen ceiling lights. I imagined being able to make out different objects and people's faces. Before I knew it, I heard the nurse's voice.

"Mr. Drumwright, you are in recovery now. Everything went well."

Surgery always seemed like I simply blinked my eyes, and then I was in recovery. Brandy had left for work shortly after I was rolled back, so I rode home with Aunt Maychelle and Aunt Sharon. We arrived at the house, and I got comfortable in my personal area in the living room. I moved my eyes around to see if I could notice any changes in my vision. Unfortunately, I couldn't get any light. Either that, or something worse had happened.

Aunt Sharon ran out and brought me back a bowl of broccoli and cheese soup and a sandwich. I finished my meal rather quickly, as I hadn't eaten anything since the night before. As I sat up to eat, I asked my aunt, "What did Dr. Schneider say about the surgery?"

She gently touched the bandage covering the left side of my face and said, "He said there was a lot of scar tissue, but your retina was in better shape than he could have anticipated. He said your retina was torn as expected, but he was able to laser it together."

I was both comforted and concerned. In my heart, I felt that my retina was in better condition than assumed but knowing that there was additional damage worried me. What if this leaves me totally blind?

In my mind, the next few weeks would be critical. It was the moment of truth.

Would my prayers be answered? And if so, to what extent?

Would God fully or partially restore my health and sight?

How many revisions would I be forced to make in my life so that I could resume as a functional contributor to society.

Or would I need to learn how to ask for and receive help from others?

My vantage point on life was forever changed. It was still undetermined just how different things would actually be.

RE-VISION

Part Two

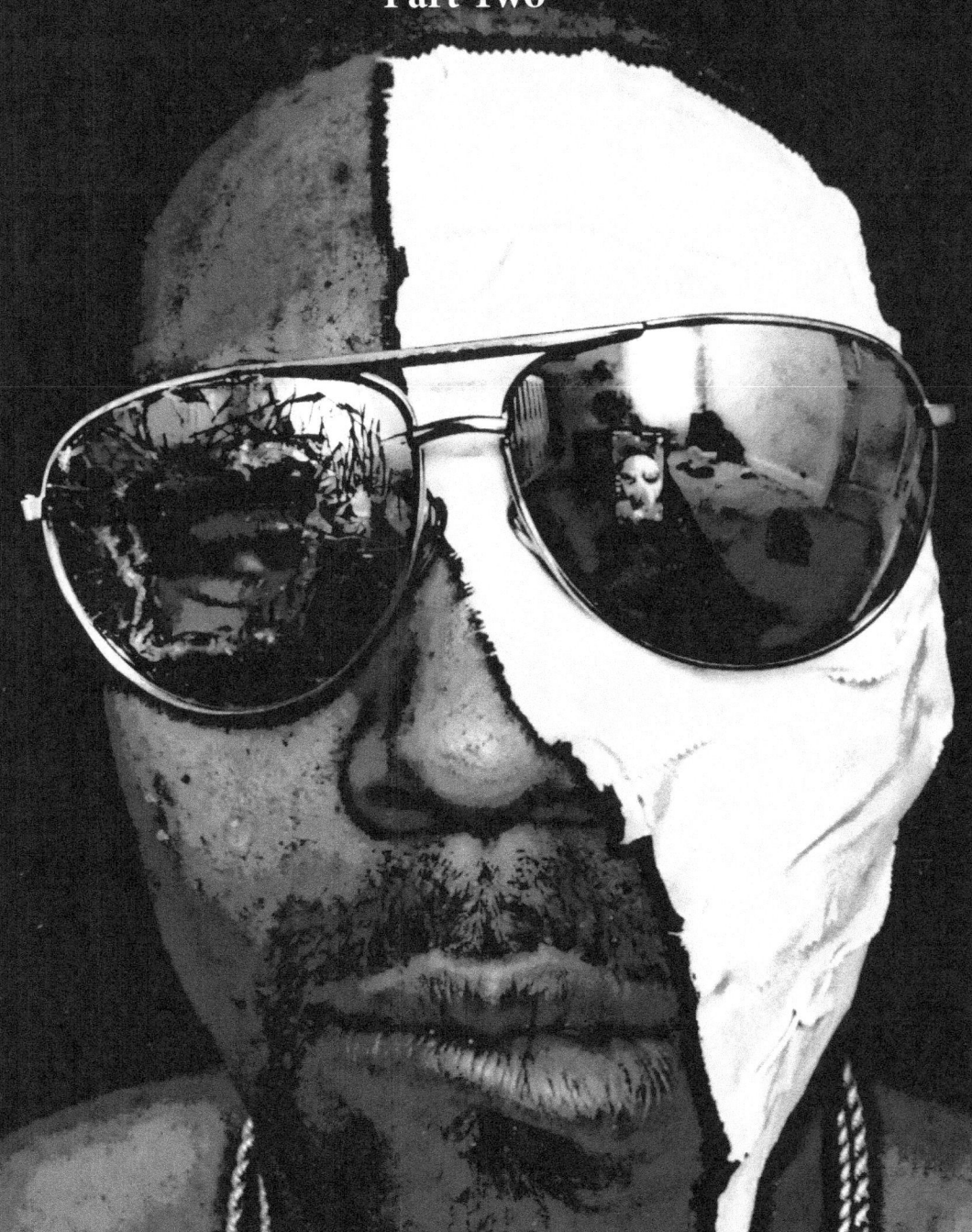

Chapter 29
The Leather Couch

"You're going through a lot, Daniel," my therapist said as I sat on the leather couch in his office. "Whether you realize it or not, hope is like money. You build up hope, and you spend it. I would say that right now you feel like hope is depleted. Would that be accurate?"

I nodded my head in agreement. It was exactly how I felt; depleted of all hope. I no longer measured time in days, and I was beginning to settle into a new normal. It had been 16 weeks since I lost my vision and about a month since the surgery on my left eye which yielded nothing more than minimal light reception. Waiting with the hope that things would get better eventually turned into just waiting. I felt isolated as life went on for everyone else.

While I still had a desire to fix my sight issues, the more reasonable thing for me to do was to learn how to keep moving forward in spite of them. It was time to properly mourn my losses, and then chart a course for the new path that I found myself on. I still had plenty of things that deserved my attention, such as: gain enough sight to return to work and finish grad school, plan the perfect marriage proposal, get stable and strong enough to return to my workouts at the gym, and regain as much independence as possible. I knew the road I was setting out on would be long and tough; not only for me, but for all of those who were on the journey with me.

It didn't help that things with Brandy were getting a little rocky.

"How is your girlfriend? How is her son?" the therapist asked me.

"She's good. Supporting me throughout it all," I replied.

I heard him scribbling on his notepad, and then he asked, "So, what have you all discussed about the future? Is she optimistic about your recovery? Have you discussed how you both will adjust to your new challenges?"

I began to explain that a spat between Brandy and me was actually one of the reasons I came to therapy in the first place. As a speech therapist, she understood the value of seeking professional help when facing challenges beyond one's ability to handle alone.

"As supportive and positive as she is, the accumulation of her normal responsibilities and caring for me has left her emotionally spent," I explained. "Not to mention, I'm constantly doing things to drive her crazy. For instance, one day I sent out a false alarm when I couldn't find Minx."

"I hope that means you found her," the doctor replied about the dog, as we both began to chuckle.

I was responsible for Minx while Brandy was at work, so we spent lots of time together. Like with humans, too much time together can drive anyone up a wall. Especially when it's a six-month-old puppy that hasn't been potty trained. I stepped in dog urine or poop on more than a handful of occasions. I guess that's easy to do when you are newly blind, but it seemed as if Minx purposefully left her piles of relief right in my path. Eventually, I lost it.

I proceeded to tell my therapist the whole story.

"I went off on the dog," I told my therapist. "I was sick of the shit. Literally. So, I scolded her, and then I went outside to relax on Brandy's back deck for hours. When I returned inside, I couldn't find her. I cursed the dog while I searched the entire house (as well as I could). After feeling around the master bathroom, I came across her empty collar, which had a charm attached that I could hear jingle as she moved. Brandy had given her a bath the night before and didn't put her collar back on. So, I couldn't see or hear her. That's when I went into panic mode. I thought Minx might have followed me outside and roamed off. I felt my way back to the deck, calling for her, but had no luck. An hour after I noticed she was missing – and as bad as I wanted to avoid it – I called Brandy to let her know."

"Brandy made record time getting home from work. She didn't even greet me when she walked through the garage door. As soon as she called out for her, Minx strolled down the steps. She had hidden under Blake's bed after I cursed her for stepping in her shit and would not come out until she knew it was safe."

"Bitch," I asserted. My therapist and I both chuckled as I completed the story.

As comical as the story about the dog was, there was more brewing beneath the surface between Brandy and me. This was the final straw in a series of events that resulted in conversations where we discussed our once-promising future. As one would imagine, I hadn't been my normal self, and my confidence had begun to waver. That evening, Brandy sat down with me and expressed her concerns. She said that my tone in our discussions had become less hopeful. My outlook was tanking, and she was on the receiving end of my bad attitude. The people who were closest to me unfortunately got the worst of me, and that was totally unfair.

"We decided we needed space to assess everything and consider the challenges we faced," I told my therapist.

I tried to be as self-sufficient as possible so Brandy had minimal worries, but she had become more solemn, and I felt guilty and responsible for her pain. I didn't want that for her. I didn't want any of this. I felt like a burden and I started to beat myself up for everything that was going on. Though I was elated to be with Brandy, she seemed distant and unexcited. Our conversations had become very short and the time we spent together felt forced. Even when we went to bed, we hardly touched each other. Our relationship lacked the energy I had grown accustomed to.

"I decided to spend less time at Brandy's house so she could have a break from the added worries she had inherited," I told my therapist. "As disappointed as I was about this, I knew it was necessary." When we were falling in love, we were so carefree. But all of that had changed.

Who wants to be with a blind man with leukemia and diabetes? I asked myself.

Brandy could have anyone. The last thing I want is someone to be with me out of pity.

I got really emotional as I sat in my therapist's office. He put tissue in my hand and asked, "What else did you say in response to the separation?"

Without raising my head, I replied. "I said 'okay, I understand.'"

"Daniel, do you know why you come to a therapist?" he asked.

I thought that was a weird question considering he was a therapist.

"You come for several reasons," he continued. "Most importantly, you come to recharge. You come to decompress. And you come to gain clarity. You seldom solve your problems here. This is where you come to make sense of them. I'm not suggesting anything as it pertains to the two of you. I just see what kind of man you are. You want to take care of everything and everyone. I know you are giving each other time, but you may want to stress your commitment to her."

I sat up and replied, "I don't want to be a burden and I definitely don't want charity. It's as simple as that."

I didn't admit this to my therapist, but my pride wouldn't allow me to beg for understanding and consideration. Why should I have to ask for something that I felt I had earned up to this point? My therapist and I both agreed that I was being my own antagonist. I knew I would have to pick myself up and show Brandy I was all the man she needed.

Chapter 30
Party of 1

After a few weeks of staying at my own home, I was consumed by my thoughts and became obsessed over living the life I dreamed of. Brandy, Blake and I still spent time together, but not regularly waking up to them became a hard reminder of my extenuating circumstances. I was being forced to modify the plans I had for myself, and I didn't know how to deal with the uncertain future that I faced. And it was entirely too late to look back. I was intimidated by my condition and just wanted the mental anguish to end.

One Monday morning – after having spent the weekend with Brandy – I was alone at her home. I went onto her back deck for my daily pow wow with myself, God and whoever else was listening. This day was different because I took a necktie with me and fitted it to my neck. I removed it and stood in the chair next to one of the posts that held up the gazebo. I felt around the inside of the gazebo and found a hook that previously had been used to hang decorations. I took the long end of the tie and tied it to the hook. Testing the strength of the hook and tie, I held on to the tie with my hands and swung from it. It didn't shred at all, and the hook was still in place.

I sat back down to wrap my head around what I was doing.

Could I really hang myself here?

Would this fix anything or make life harder for Brandy, my dad, my brothers, my friends, and my family?

If I make this decision, will God understand and have mercy on my soul?

I knew the answers, but still I contemplated moving forward with my actions. Then, I stood up in the chair again and slipped my head through the open end of the tie. I was nervous and out of breath, like I was running for my life, but I was really running from my life. My heart was racing. My adrenaline was pumping.

As I stood in the unsteady chair, I kept seeing an image of my mom in my thoughts. She was in a crowd of people in an amusement park. She stood looking in my direction as the mass of people moved about. She stared at me with sadness in her eyes. I couldn't let that image go and I began to feel discouraged. I knew she would be hurt and disappointed in me if I gave up, and I wasn't ready to spend eternity knowing that.

C'mon. This ain't what you want, Daniel. Not for you, and not for anyone, I said to myself.

I didn't want to die. I just wanted things to be better than they were. I wanted to live again.

I stood in the chair holding the tie around my neck as it hung from the hook. I hung my head and began to remove myself from the home-made noose. I didn't want to leave any evidence of what I had just done for Brandy to find, so I began to remove the hanging tie as best I could. From what felt like right beside me, a voice called out to me.

"Hey, bro! What you doing?" Brandy's neighbor said all of a sudden. His broken English startled me, causing me to lose my footing. I came crashing to the deck with an unbelievable force. Because of my sight limitations, I wasn't able to gauge my distance from the ground nor brace myself. This fall gave new meaning to the phrase "pain in the ass."

"Damn, man! You okay?" he said as he put his hands under my arm pit to help me up. A native of a small Asian village where nothing was private, Brandy's neighbor's behavior always seemed intrusive. Otherwise, he was a nice guy.

Had he been watching me the whole time? How much did he see?

I couldn't help but wonder if my flirt with death had been witnessed by anyone else. That would have been embarrassing. I was already disappointed in myself for even going so far down that path. As a man, I felt like it was my role to be strong. But ultimately, I knew that hurting myself in a moment of weakness would do nothing but hurt everyone else in my life.

The neighbor kept me company for about an hour, which I was grateful for. He asked how my eyes were and told me he would find me new eyes one day. He was definitely drunk. I chuckled and thanked him.

As he sat beside me drinking a beer and smoking a cigarette, I thought about what I had just done; I contemplated quitting life. I considered taking matters into my own hands to end my pain. The thought had crossed my mind over a span of a couple of days. But mostly it was an impulsive idea that overwhelmed me within a couple of hours. The possibility of being blind, depending on others for the rest of my life and possibly losing my woman made me feel like less of a man. It was a truth that I didn't want to live. And I didn't see any hope of things changing or moving in a positive direction.

I didn't tell a soul about what I did that day, not even my therapist. Subconsciously, I hoped that never bringing it up again would help me forget that it happened at all. Unfortunately, it wasn't the last time I had thoughts of ending it all by taking my own life.

Chapter 31
Liquidated Damages

Living with low vision was a huge adjustment to say the least. One of the biggest changes to my lifestyle was the inability to return to work. As a result, I officially began receiving disability benefits.

My supervisor in the Mayor's Office had been extremely supportive during my illness, but it eventually became apparent to everyone that I would not be able to resume my position while the current administration was in place. Any recovery that allowed me to return to a normal work environment was likely to happen long after my boss's term was over. And the next mayor would surely bring in their own – new – team. It was painful coming to the realization that my time in the Mayor's Office was over. Not to mention the financial strain that resulted from a reduced income.

After exhausting all of my vacation days with my employer, I received short-term disability for a period of time. After that came long-term disability where I received income that was 60 percent of my normal salary. The last stop on the disability benefits line was receiving Social Security Disability Insurance benefits distributed by the federal government from which I received an even smaller income each month.

Going on disability was a big deal, but because my health was taking up most of my attention, I didn't fully absorb how significantly it would affect my ability to function and move forward. The whole process was somewhat of a blur taking place in the background of me losing my sight. My oncologist, Dr. Erter, signed the forms for my disability approval, and my Aunt Maychelle did most of the heavy lifting to get all my paperwork submitted to the appropriate entities so that funds continued to flow into my bank account. She kept me abreast of the specifics, but unfortunately, it came in one ear and left immediately out of the other. As long as my bills were getting paid, and David and my dad had access to money to manage our condo, I knew everything else would be taken care of.

Getting assistance from the government didn't bother me. But, it irked me that I was not able to earn the amount of money that I was used to making. I knew that, eventually, life would pick back up, and the insurance benefits I was receiving wouldn't be enough to sustain my desired lifestyle. I had built up a decent nest egg over the span of my career up to that point, but a major health crisis like this was no match for the savings I had accumulated.

The financial impact of my illness was an added layer of stress that I knew would eventually require my full attention. But at the time, it was in the background, quietly lingering, waiting for its moment to raise hell in the future.

Although I couldn't return to work, I still had to figure out how to try to get back on my feet somehow. If I was going to live a full life, it was time to start learning how to do so.

A representative from the Department of Human Services came to my condo and conducted a home assessment. She brought a handful of items that would help me use appliances and complete household chores. Vocational rehabilitation helps disabled individuals to adjust to their new circumstances and manage everyday tasks with easy-to-use equipment and minimal assistance.

She placed silicone pieces over the start and power buttons on the microwave and stove. Then she placed them on the washer and dryer so that I could find the settings. She brought a talking clock and protective cutting glove. She told me a few additional items would arrive by mail. And, sure enough, about a week after her visit, a package arrived.

I unpacked it and felt around the medium-sized box to determine what was sent. I found an electronic talking labeler to tag different items, a magnifier and a talking keychain.

There was one more small item that came in the package. The compact cardboard package was slightly heavy and sounded like metal. I unpacked it. The five metal ends snapped together as I held the handle from one side. It was a walking stick for blind people. My attitude quickly shifted. I imagined walking up the street with the stick trying to find my way with people gawking as they drove by. Even though I wouldn't be able to see them looking, I imagined what their expressions would be.

I opened the back door and crossed the deck. I felt for the rail and tossed the walking stick off the deck toward the wired fence that ran through the backyard. I heard it strike the tree branches and fall to the ground short of the fence. I didn't care where it landed, but it wasn't about to go back inside with me.

A day or two later, the maintenance man who cut the grass for the complex found it out back. And when he discovered it was mine, I told him to leave it on the deck.

I prided myself on being strong. I was taught at an early age that men are supposed to show little emotion, and that being perceived as "soft" is not okay. I didn't want to be vulnerable, so I acted as if most things didn't bother me, but emotions cannot be concealed forever. In my mind, relying on a walking stick was admitting defeat. During my next visit with my therapist, I told him about my lack of interest in using it.

"I think I will get enough vision back, so really, I won't need it," I said as I tried to justify my actions. "Why learn to use something that I probably won't have to use? I'm not using that thing unless I just have to."

I heard my therapist take a sip of his drink before he asked, "Does the thought of using that stick bother you or make you feel vulnerable? Do you talk about how you feel with anyone else? Brandy or your family?"

"Truth is, I am afraid that my real feelings will scare everyone, especially Brandy," I confessed. "I know we are talking about someone I want to marry, but I haven't been able to get over myself."

He replied, "I understand it's difficult to share your feelings, but I think Brandy would really want to know. As your partner, she deserves to know how you're feeling. It affects her and your relationship. Especially, if you plan to marry her. She will be okay with whatever you feel comfortable sharing, but I think it's better to do so than not."

With everything that had been going on with us, the last thing I wanted to do was to be needy or spread darkness over her light. So, I left my therapist's advice on the couch in his office.

**

I exited the therapist's office, and my brother Darrell was waiting to take me home. He asked me questions about my sessions, but was never intrusive. He kept it simple. We talked about other things, like relationships and family. He always had hilarious stories and experiences to share. We often spoke about our childhood and how our experiences had motivated our life decisions. Because of our relationship as brothers, conversations about religion and spirituality had a unique and honest tone. And he always had good advice, as you would expect from an older brother.

Because he was my pastor, maybe I should have sought more spiritual understanding from him during this time. I told myself I was protecting my brother by suppressing my emotions. But honestly, I wasn't sure I could deal with the emotions, and I wasn't ready to accept where I was.

After Darrell helped me inside, I sat in the living room and turned on the television. Before leaving, he made sure I was comfortable and gave me a kiss on the head, like he did when I was a little kid. I sat on the couch, ate my food, and listened to a broadcast of a church service on the television.

"Miracles are happening every day!" the minister exclaimed as the congregation reacted with excitement and joy.

I said aloud, "I wonder where my miracle is at?"

I had memorized where each number was located on the remote control, so I used my muscle memory to turn the channel to ESPN. I listened to Jalen Rose talk about Steph Curry's performance the night before. I thought about what I'd normally be doing during this time.

I'm supposed to be at the gym hooping, but no. God got me stuck in the house eating a chicken biscuit and listening to Jalen Rose's ass, I said to myself.

Whether I was at my condo, my aunt and uncle's home, or at Brandy's home, the monotony of being stationary began to wear on me. Still, I couldn't find the energy to break out of this rut. I was occasionally invited to outings with my family and friends, but I always felt out of place. I didn't want to be seen that way and I didn't want to be anywhere if I couldn't see. More than anything, I couldn't accept that I was limited in how much control I had over my circumstances. I questioned my ability to take care of Brandy and Blake. I knew I had to find a way, though. I didn't have a choice, and I didn't want any other choice. The control I was used to having was gone. I now had to rely on faith. I had to trust.

***

During my time apart from Brandy, I tried not to bother her with questions about us. I wanted her to feel at peace, but I also wanted her to miss me like I missed her. Luckily for me, I could tell that she did.

During one of our routine evening conversations, she asked about my day and how I had been feeling. I asked her the same.

"Everything is going good. I miss you so much, though," she said, with a quiver in her voice. She began to cry, and we expressed how grateful we were for each other.

"Not one time have you pressured me or made me feel bad for anything. And I have been beating myself up for not being more understanding…" she said.

I interrupted before she could finish her statement. "You have been more understanding than many people could have ever been. You have supported me like a true partner is supposed to. And you don't have to. We're not married, so you have nothing binding you to me. It's me that should be apologizing."

I told her my pride prevented me from talking about my worries and concerns with her. I told her how I didn't want her to feel burdened by me. I also expressed how dedicated to her I would be and how I would never allow my physical ailment to prevent me from being my best.

"It doesn't matter if I get no more vision back. I will be the sexiest and most fine blind guy in life," I said jokingly. We laughed and cried, and we talked about life and how we would adjust. The tension I felt trying to avoid bothering Brandy with this conversation was immediately alleviated.

"So, whenever you decide to propose, just know I want you home with me permanently," she said.

With delight, I replied, "Deal."

While the conversation gave me the self-esteem boost I needed, I was now on the hook. I would have to challenge myself to stay positive and remain hopeful. Not just for me, but for Brandy. For everyone. I was up for the challenge, but deep down I knew my patience and poise would be pushed to the limits.

Chapter 32
Magnified Proposal

Though doubt often found its way into my psyche, I was motivated to believe in myself again. My vision was slightly improving, and my family encouraged me to try using a magnifying glass to assist me. I imagined I looked pretty silly holding a big magnifying glass up to my eye, but it actually helped me read more lines on the eye chart and sort of follow sports on TV. My confidence had also been elevated now that I had been given the reassurance from Brandy concerning our future and I wanted to show her that I was all in. I had gained a small bit of ground. Now, I had to figure out how I was going to propose.

I sat down with some of my Dunnies on a Saturday afternoon and told them I needed their help pulling this off. It had been five months since I showed them the engagement rings, and it was now time to take the next step.

"We got you, Dunny. Whatever you need," they said as we ate brunch at a local restaurant. My original plan was to propose outside of Public Square in Downtown Nashville. I had surveyed the location several times because the Mayor's Office was there. Out front were water fountains that spouted from the ground and led to a sidewalk where people could gather. I planned on leading Brandy to this location after dinner and surprising her with family awaiting.

I had produced a song specifically for our engagement before I got sick. I had it all planned out, but with my recent health issues – and lack of time – it felt nearly impossible to execute the way I had imagined. With the help of my friends, we decided that the downtown pedestrian bridge – that connected 3rd Avenue South and Nissan Stadium (the home field of the Tennessee Titans) – was the ideal location to pull off the proposal.

"I will get her family and friends to meet us there. I'll have Brandy's sister, Pinky, get signs made so everyone can hold them," I said as we ate brunch. They suggested we do a "Sushi Saturdays" outing near the bridge so it would be easy to lure Brandy up there.

"She'll never see it coming," my friend Theo said.

"Hell, neither will I," I joked.

This was one of the first times I had been out since not being able to get around on my own. It felt good to be around friends and not think about everything that was going on.

"It's time! On to the next spot! Let's roll," Decosta exclaimed as we finished our meal and prepared to head to the next location. He had assumed the role of "Sushi," the orchestrator of "Sushi Saturdays." Theo knew the bartender at a nearby eatery, so we patronized that location for about an hour. Several people we all knew met us there. It had been a while since I had been with several of them. They all spoke positive and uplifting words to me as we caught up on life.

***

In the weeks leading up to the proposal, I thought about how I was going to ask Brandy to be my wife. I imagined leaving brunch from a downtown restaurant and her meeting me on 3rd Avenue at the entrance of the pedestrian bridge. I imagined her seeing the commotion of our friends and family standing on the bridge waving signs and balloons, cheering while I got down on one knee and pulled out the ring. I imagined the perfect execution of a well-thought-out plan.

I worked closely with Pinky to think through the details.

"I looked online to research getting an umbrella made for the proposal," she updated me during one of our planning calls. "But it would need to be a really big umbrella to get all of the words 'Brandy, Will You Marry Me?' on it. We could go with multiple smaller umbrellas, but that could cost over $350. Are you sure you want to go that route?"

"For some umbrellas?! Why so much?!" I asked her. I wasn't too concerned about the umbrellas not working out, as long as we made other provisions. I had a vision that I wanted to create. Pinky promised to check a few other vendors, but I assured her that signs would be fine if the umbrellas were a no-go. I asked Brandy's friend, Monica, to contact others and let them know the plan; Brandy would pick me up downtown after I spent the afternoon with my Dunnies, and we'd lure her to the bridge where everyone would be waiting. I even called her friends from college to give them the opportunity to be there. I did all I could to make sure all the logistics were in place. Now, I had to count on everyone else to do their part.

***

The morning of the proposal, I woke up early to pack my duffle bag. I made sure I had my slacks, dress shirt, and a nice pair of loafers to change into for the big moment. I had hidden the rings in the back of Brandy's closet the week before so I didn't forget to bring them to her home that weekend. I retrieved them and stuffed them deep into my backpack. Brandy often went through my bags to make sure I had everything I needed, so I didn't want her to stumble across them. Then, I went downstairs to the kitchen to make breakfast. The aroma of bacon and eggs drifted upstairs and awoke Brandy and Blake. They came downstairs to find me in the kitchen with the magnifying glass up to my left eye and a cooking fork in my right hand.

"Well, good morning sleepy heads. I have bacon, eggs, pancakes, and fruit for everyone," I said with delight. The dog stood on her hind legs and pressed her front paws against my calves. I reached down and petted her and said, "Yes, I got you some bacon, too."

Brandy grabbed me from behind and said, "You are awesome."

The morning started off perfectly. We ate, talked about the school year coming to a close for Blake, and planned a trip to Minneapolis to visit her family for the Fourth of July. Brandy inviting me to go was reassuring that the proposal had God's certified approval.

I took a shower after breakfast and got all my things together for Decosta to pick me up. As I waited for him to arrive, I sat on the couch going through what I was going to say and do when Brandy got to the bridge. I played it over and over in my head.

When Decosta rang the doorbell, I said a short prayer before getting up to answer.

God, it's time. Be with me as I make this step. Help me find a way to make her proud to be with me and make this special. Amen.

I hopped up and opened the door. Decosta walked in to greet Blake and Brandy, and then grabbed my bag to take to his car. I kissed Brandy and told her I would see her around 4:00 p.m. We headed to his vehicle and left for his downtown apartment to pregame and wait on our other friends to go eat.

As everyone arrived, they greeted me with excitement and congratulated me. I was encouraged throughout the day about the decision I was about to make, as we patronized several local businesses and enjoyed the great spring weather. At 2:30 p.m. we all headed back to Decosta's apartment so I could get dressed for the big moment.

I ironed my clothing and monitored the time using voice commands on my phone. JW handed me a drink, and we all gathered in the living area where my cousin Ryan made a toast. I was grateful for all the support I was getting. After finishing my drink, I got dressed and we headed to the car. The bridge was only five minutes away, so we got to 3rd Ave South at 3:15 p.m. I called Brandy to check in and see where she was.

"Hey baby. I am headed to pick up something to eat for Blake, and then I will be on my way."

I had already planned for Blake to go with her mom after the proposal, so everything was on track.

"Man, this is not the business," Decosta said while turning into a parking lot near the bridge.

"What's up? You can't find a parking spot?" I asked as I couldn't tell what caused him to respond this way.

He exhaled and stated, "There is a bunch of people up on the bridge. There are chairs and tables up there. It looks like a wedding or something."

I didn't find his comments funny, so I said with sarcasm, "Well, they're gonna have to move! I got something to do!"

His silence was a sign of seriousness, and I was completely dumbfounded. I held my magnifying glass up in an attempt to see what was going on. Decosta tapped me on the arm and said, "The bridge is the other way."

I quickly turned in the opposite direction. I obviously couldn't see anything, but I heard a group of people walking by the car say, "Oh wow! They are having a wedding on the bridge! That's so beautiful." Anger and frustration quickly washed over me.

"Man, what in the hell?! They would be up there when I'm trying to propose!" I exclaimed.

Decosta quickly attempted to calm me. He grabbed my shoulder and said, "Aye, we are gonna do this. Don't worry, we are gonna figure this out. We still got time."

As he finished his comment, another group of pedestrians walked by our vehicle. A female voice said, "Oh wow! Look at the wedding."

My emotions got the best of me and I let more expletives fly out of my mouth. Decosta let out a slight laugh.

At that moment, Pinky called me.

"Hey brother! What's going on at the bridge? They won't even let me walk across." She was on the opposite side of the bridge and was forced to drive around to meet us. I told her a wedding was happening, and I didn't know what else to do.

"Brother, don't sweat it. We are going to make this happen. Where is Brandy?"

I called Brandy again to see where she was. She was now 20 minutes away, giving us little time to improvise. Several of our friends and family started to arrive. Decosta helped me out of the car to greet them and let them know what was going on. They all tried to think of an alternative setup to quickly arrange before she arrived.

The confusion and commotion started to damper my mood, so I asked Decosta to let me back in the car so I could think. As he closed the door and walked away, my eyes began to water. I had prayed a lot in the past several weeks for this moment. I didn't understand how God could allow this to happen, knowing all that I had been through; knowing all the planning we did to make this a beautiful moment. I still believed God wouldn't allow this moment to be ruined.

C'mon, now. I can't tell You how helpless I feel right now. God, I'm counting on You. I don't know how to pull this off, now. I've always been clutch, but I can't do what I used to do. So, I'm asking You for two things. First, I need this bridge to clear in the next 10 minutes. I don't care how; I just need it done. Secondly, I need…

I was interrupted by someone opening the door. Before they could say a word, I said, "I'm praying. Just wait."

I paused for a moment and continued my prayer.

Second, I need You to give me enough sight to get around on my own. I know I have asked You for this a million times, but I am so serious. I need my independence. I need to feel like a man. I need to show everyone, especially Brandy, that I am whole, regardless how well I see. I just need to be able to see something. Amen.

I finished my prayer and assumed my cousin was there. I held my magnifying glass up to see his silhouette.

"The bridge is clearing. They're finished with the wedding and the procession just walked off. They are packing up chairs and everything," he said to me.

I paused and wiped my eyes. I lifted my head and said, "Thank You. Thank You for hearing me."

Decosta guided me to the bridge where I met back up with our family and friends. A mini celebration ensued on the sidewalk. They all knew how much this meant to me, and they were more than supportive.

By this time, Brandy called to let me know she was near and to ask if Decosta could bring me to her car so she didn't have to get out. Decosta expressed that he wanted her to come up to get a female's perspective on the backdrop for a video that some of our cohorts were shooting. She reluctantly agreed.

She parked near the 2nd Avenue overpass and walked up a set of steps that led to the top of the bridge. Before she could get to the bridge, Blake came running up the steps. As he got there, he saw several familiar faces and questioned what was going on. We hushed him, but before we could get him to join the group, he went running back down the steps to meet his mom.

"Momma, there is a bunch of people up here. Auntie Pinky and Nannie," he said to her. I almost had a heart attack when I heard him. Before they came into view, I heard Brandy say, "I wonder what they are doing down here."

With the magnifying glass up to my eye, I waited for Brandy to come around the corner. She was about to greet me when she apparently saw everyone behind me. She let out a big scream and said, "I should have known! I was like, 'what in the hell is Decosta talking about? And why is Pinky up here?'"

I got down on one knee with the magnifying glass in my hand. I looked towards her, as best I could and said, "Would you do me the honor of being my wife?"

"Yes, of course!" she quickly replied. After placing the engagement ring on her hand, I stood and pulled her close to kiss her. Our group of family and friends caused pandemonium as we embraced each other. I could hear strangers cheer at the end of the bridge as we made our way down the incline. I carried my head high as we exited the bridge and gathered on 3rd Avenue South. Brandy continued to kiss me on the cheek as we stood making plans for the evening. I turned to face my bride-to-be with little to no sight. I didn't need a magnifying glass to see her smile. I felt it.

Chapter 33
Pulitzer's Surprise

With new motivation and a rejuvenated spirit, I set my sights on re-establishing my independence, becoming more self-sufficient, and adding value to my new home with Brandy and Blake.

With practically no sight, I took on the responsibility of washing dishes, cleaning the downstairs bathroom, and making sure the dog was walked every day. I tried to make myself available for anything I could do to help take the load off of Brandy.

I wanted to take the initiative to work on my health – mental and physical – so that I could be the best man for my family and future wife.

I asked my father to take me to a low vision specialist so that I could have the little vision that I did have assessed. I had some reservation, considering that vision in my left eye had gotten no sharper than 20/400 in my five appointments since the surgery. But my insurance covered the visit, so I decided to go.

Dr. Pulitzer, the low vision specialist, was an older and very friendly gentleman. His voice was warm and calm like a grandfather's. He had been a low vision specialist for decades. I caught him up on my circumstances and how I ended up in his office. He put me through a barrage of tests to assess my vision. I surprised myself, as I scored higher than I thought I would.

The specialist put a contraption on my face that had several different lens slots. He began putting in lenses and asking me whether I could see the chart. I couldn't see anything and didn't expect to, but he continued to change out different lenses. After changing out the lens settings several times, I could make out some of the letters on the wall. Though they were larger print, I was quite excited that my left eye was able to make out the image.

"Alright. I got your fitting for distance. Let's get you fitted for reading glasses."

We took a short break so the doctor could jot down notes and set up the other equipment. He positioned a scope that had several lens settings. Excited, I placed my head in between the face plate and began peering at a smudged image. He flipped through lenses and asked me to let him know when the image became clearer. We eventually got to a setting where I could actually see the small print.

Things were moving so quickly that I didn't have time to process what was actually happening. The specialist had me sit back while he set a pair of lenses in adjustable frames. He placed the frames over my eyes and put a piece of paper in my hands.

"Okay, read this line here," he stated as he placed his finger on the paper where the sentence began. While I could tell the print was rather small, I could read it with ease.

"Okay. Now read this line."

I struggled to read the words but eventually got through the line. I was disappointed in myself until I heard the chuckle.

"That was 8-point font. You were able to read 8-point font. Dad, you see that right there?" he asked my father as we all sat in awe.

I could hear my dad whimper, trying to hold back tears. The specialist removed the frames from my eyes and my poor vision returned instantly. I turned toward the smudged blob that was my father's figure, and reached for him. He grabbed my hand, squeezed it tight and started thanking God. I smiled, thinking the same thing. The specialist had set up my distance vision setting in a pair of frames so that we could test them.

"Look out that glass door and tell me what you can see."

I could see the cars lined up in the parking lot. I looked further out and could tell cars were driving up and down the road. I could see a group of people walking through the parking lot towards the building. My vision definitely wasn't clear, but I could see more than I had been able to in six months. And without a magnifying glass. It literally took my breath away. As I stared out the glass door in awe, the specialist placed his hand on my shoulder and spoke.

"I have seen a lot of eyes in my 40-plus years of work. You definitely have a ways to go, but looking at how your vision is responding to the surgeries and the lens settings, I believe you will be able to function well with glasses. You might surprise me and make an even more remarkable recovery, but just know it will likely take some time. Be patient and faithful. Follow the doctor's orders, of course, and we will see what God has in store for you."

It was reassuring to know that he was a spiritual man. I needed the constant reminders to stay focused on the light at the end of the tunnel. The specialist and his assistant helped me pick out two sets of frames: one for distance and one for reading. Both pairs would take three to four weeks to arrive.

I told him that Brandy and I were planning a trip to Minnesota. It was her Uncle Buck's birthday and we were going to attend the celebration. This was a big deal for me since we were newly engaged and it would be the first time I met some of her family members. I asked if there was any way the glasses could be rushed.

"I can't be sure they will arrive before you leave, but I will definitely put a rush on it," he reassured me. That's all I could ask for. As we finished up, Dr. Pulitzer left me with a scripture that he believed I should hold close during my journey.

"Jeremiah 29:11. For I know the plans I have for you, declares the LORD, plans to prosper you and not to harm you, plans to give you hope and a future."

I walked out of the office with so much hope. For the first time in what seemed like forever, I was able to see detail. It was like someone opened the door to a dark room.

I sat in the car with my dad and could tell he was still quite emotional about seeing me read. He began to open up candidly.

"You know, I have been dealing with all sorts of emotions. I have been angry, sad, hurt, but seeing you read…" His words trailed off as he tried to maintain his composure.

Hearing him say that meant more than I think either of us understood. My father had not come to the hospital for any of my surgeries. I wanted him to be there, but because I had so much support from other family members, I don't think he felt like he needed to be there. I could tell how hurt he was to see his child's life in the balance. Not being able to do anything about it had to be even worse. Because my father had never dealt well with difficult and emotional matters, it was easier for him to keep a safe distance during this time. I almost felt like the health issues I faced couldn't compare to the heartbreak and trauma my father experienced in his life. I heard lots of stories about being raised in the projects in the 1950s and 1960s. I learned about the physical and emotional abuse he faced as a child which led to a lifetime of depression and mental anguish. I hadn't considered any of this when I thought about my dad's reluctance to be present. I tried to conceal my emotions in his presence, but deep down I was bothered by his absence. I was sure he could sense this. I began to feel guilty for being so self-absorbed and upset since the beginning of my health issues. I just hoped he understood my pain, as I had tried to understand his.

My father apologized and reinforced his support for all three of his sons. None of that mattered anymore, though. All that mattered was that he was with me now.

"You'll get those glasses, and we'll go driving," he joked with me.

"Yeah, I'm not sure y'all want me on the road quite yet," I joked back.

We went to McDonald's before heading home. We sat inside and talked for a while, mostly reminiscing on my childhood. We talked about fond moments, like me growing up playing sports and my mom and Aunt Maychelle being the loudest people cheering at the field. We also talked about some of the harder memories, like my mom's passing and some volatile moments my father had in my childhood. On one occasion, David was left downtown after a Titans football game. To say that my father erupted was an understatement. In the past, it had been really difficult for my dad to talk about these moments, but not so much this day.

"You know, I have tried to forget some of those things. I'm ashamed of myself for getting that upset, but I didn't handle my emotions well back then. I was stressed, dealing with trying to make a living. I was being pulled in different directions for assistance. And I was dealing with the scars of being a child of a 13-year-old mother who faced her own challenges. My father was in jail, while my brothers and sisters had a father. That's not an excuse, but it definitely didn't help. Darrell has talked to me about some of the moments I had even before you and David were here, and I have to face them, knowing that no matter how much I want to sweep them under a rug and forget they happened; they did. The fact that you all remember those moments," he began to tear up again. "I'm sorry, Daniel."

I smiled and gave him a kiss on the cheek. I'm not sure I have ever been prouder to call him "Daddy."

I returned home feeling like we shared a moment we would never forget. Reading those lines in front of him did more good than I could have imagined. The dialogue that later ensued at McDonald's was more heart-felt than any conversation I could remember. More than anything, it was healing for both of our spirits.

As he helped me inside, my dad hugged me. "Daniel, I am very proud of you. You have every reason to be mad, angry and hurt, and I'm sure you are. But you handle it in a way that gives me hope and peace. Thank you."

Although my illness was causing stress for my family, it was also – in an unexpected way – bringing us closer together.

After my father left, I turned on the TV and listened to music.

***

The next few weeks would be unnerving. I prayed constantly that my glasses arrived before leaving for Minneapolis.

"Baby, I just don't want to have to be out of town without having some vision," I explained to Brandy.

She placed her hand on my leg and said, "I get that, but if they don't arrive, don't let it ruin your trip. I promise we will have a good time."

I nodded my head in agreement, but I really didn't feel that way.

"Of course, we will." I replied as I gave her a kiss.

Truth is, that I didn't want to go anywhere without the glasses. I had been given a temporary window to see the world again, and then it was put on hold. All I could think about was being able to see the bit of detail those lenses gave me. Being in a place where I had never been and not being able to admire the scenery at least was not a thrilling thought for me.

"Okay, I'm lying," I said firmly. "I really just want to see something. Anything. And I don't want to meet that side of your family and not even be able to see them. What are they going to think of me?"

I was insecure, which I felt was merited. It certainly made me feel weak. Before I knew it, I was in tears. I know Brandy wanted to be harder on me, but she knew how much of a blow to my spirit and ego this all had been.

"Baby, do you realize who you are? Your personality, your charisma, your strength, and resilience. They will feel privileged to meet someone who has dealt with what you have gone through and is still trying to live a full life. And I don't give a damn about how they think. I think you're pretty swell. What I think is all that matters." She kissed me and slapped me on the butt. I smiled.

I got more and more impatient in the days leading up to our scheduled departure. As Monday came, I grew more nervous about going on the trip without the glasses. I hadn't heard from the eye doctor about them, so my optimism and attitude tanked.

I'm gonna have to go on this trip with no glasses. This is bullshit. It's not like I should expect anything less. God, I swear You can give me a break. If I can't have them for the trip, I'm staying home. And I'm gonna lose my fiancé over this, and I'm gonna blame You.

I exclaimed while looking up to the ceiling with anger. I imagined I was looking God in the face, not at all fearing the repercussions. I had a moment of rage that came out like no other time I could remember. I have definitely been mad at God, but this was different. I breathed deeply to calm and compose my emotions. After I got ahold of myself, I began to feel remorseful.

God, I apologize. That was out of line. I'm just hurting. There's no excuse. I know. I just pray You consider my heart and not my foolish words.

God definitely knew my heart, and I didn't want to reap the consequences for speaking unfavorably to Him, but I wasn't completely sorry. A part of me was content and firm on letting Him know I was not happy with the hand I had been dealt. But I wasn't foolish enough to believe that God couldn't hear my words and respond accordingly.

Tuesday evening arrived, and I had yet to receive a call about my frames. Wednesday would be the last day I could possibly get them before we hit the road.

"Welp, I guess I'll take my blind ass on to Minneapolis," I said moping. While waiting on Brandy to get home, I lay on the couch hoping that some way I would get the call I had been waiting for. I listened to music videos on TV to pass the time.

She arrived a short time later and as usual, I put on a straight face in an attempt to hide my disappointment. It didn't take her long to sense I was feeling some type of way.

"So, I guess I won't be getting my glasses," I said as she entered the room.

She turned and gave me a white box. It was a cupcake from HomeStyle Bakery, one of Nashville's best bakeries.

"You will have them when we leave for Panama City the following week, so just try to have fun. Okay?" she asked.

I took a bite of the cupcake. White icing on white cake.

"At least I have you. And the cupcake," I said. I decided I wasn't going to be bothered by it, at least for the time being.

The next morning, Brandy and Blake left the house to start their day and I spent the rest of the morning looking for anything to keep my mind from thinking about the glasses. I felt confident they wouldn't arrive, but I was still trying to decide whether to call my doctor's office.

"I'll call them if I don't hear back by noon."

That meant I only had about a three-hour wait until it was confirmed. I was actually at peace with it all. At the end of the day, I knew that this trip wasn't about me. Brandy was taking me to meet and spend time with family she hadn't seen in forever. As much as I wanted to pout about it, I was going to have to suck it up.

For about an hour, I listened to sports news on TV where reporters were providing updates about the upcoming football season. I was elated to know I would soon be able to see live football again. About that time my phone rang, and I heard an unfamiliar voice on the other end.

"Mr. Drumwright this is Nicole, the tech for your low vision specialist."

She went on to tell me that only one pair of glasses had arrived. They were the distance glasses. I felt so many emotions at that moment. I didn't even call Brandy. I wanted to surprise her. I called David and asked him to take me to get them. He didn't say much, but I could tell he was happy and relieved. And I was relieved because going to Minnesota was something I felt I could, now, enjoy.

Chapter 34
Lil Darryl

I put on the glasses and looked at the eye chart while in the low vision specialist's office.

"You are 20/90, now. That's good," the tech said as she wrote down the results. Peering through the frames, I noticed obvious changes in clarity, but also realized that I was far from 20/20.

"How do they feel?" The tech asked with a smile.

"They are much heavier than my glasses before, but I can deal," I responded as I adjusted the frames in the mirrors. After paying $1,400 out of pocket for both pair of low vision spectacles, I was determined to make them work. I looked at my reflection and thought about all the times I cut my own hair.

That's a chore that I will have to permanently outsource, I thought.

My visual status went from "blind" to "low vision" with the help of the glasses. I quickly realized that my new frames would not be the big fix I had imagined. Everything appeared hazy, as if I was in a smoky club as the lights came on. The gray blemishes and smudges weren't clearer, either. It was as if I was looking at a large puzzle with several unfinished areas. Colors were quite muted like when a newspaper is soaked by a spilled drink.

Not to mention, there was interference in my vision, as if I was seeing a bad TV signal. None of these things were new but seemed more magnified now that I actually had some vision. Nevertheless, I was just happy to have some improved sight. I got up to walk and quickly realized I would have to get adjusted to the magnification.

"We will call you when the magnifying reading glasses arrive. I'm so happy they got here before you left."

I followed David to the car, as my eyes were still adjusting. I attached the sunglass clip-ons and gazed out the window admiring sights I had not seen in months as we traveled home. I was alleviated of much of the anxiety, as my patience had been pushed to its furthest limits. As we arrived home, I was able to walk to the front door without much assistance. I had to take my time to assure I would not trip over anything along the way. I got inside and immediately went to the bathroom to peer at my reflection.

Wow, I have put on weight, I thought while smiling. I was grinning because I actually already knew that even without the glasses. I took a step back and noticed how big my eyes looked. I immediately thought about Lil Darryl, the on-stage fictitious character that the comedian Ricky Smiley portrayed in his stand-up bit. Lil Darryl had poor vision and wore extremely thick lenses. The coincidence was I was often referred to as "Lil Darrell." Other than our height, my older brother and I favored quite a bit. I had always been proud to be referred to as "Lil Darrell," but the pop bottle-sized lenses changed all of that for me. From my perspective, there was nothing cool about these glasses, and in fact, I thought they made me look kinda goofy just like Lil Darryl.

My smile quickly vanished.

I went to the living room couch, where I had spent so much of the past seven months and sent pictures of myself in my new frames to my friends and family. After using the magnifying glass to help send the text, I stood up to take the dog outside. As I opened the front door, the sunlight hit my eye, and bursts of lightning and twinkling flares saturated my vision. This would happen at times, but it seemed more intense this day.

After about a minute of being dazed and impaired, my vision stabilized and I was able to proceed forward. Minx, excited to be outside, tugged the leash with all of the might she had in her seven-pound body. The sun was unforgiving on my reconstructed retinas. I attached the clip-on sunglasses the tech gave me to block out the sun. This helped and impaired me all at the same time. While they blocked the sun, it was evident I would need a lighter-shaded lens, as they also impeded my vision.

While I was focusing so much on my vision, or lack thereof, Minx had set her sights on a group of kids. Without warning, she took off toward them, yanking the leash out of my hand. I lifted the clip-ons and took off after her. Luckily, I was able to see her from behind. After allowing her to greet the teens, we retreated back toward the house. Instead of putting my clip-ons back on, I held my opposite hand over my eyes to shield them from the sun.

As we entered the house, the same bolts of lightning and flashes of electricity filled my vision. The transitions from light and dark seemed to be the cause of this. As my vision readjusted from being outside, I noticed a glare that gleamed off of the pattern of the suds of silicone oil that was used to stabilize my retinas. I sat back in that same spot I had grown accustomed to sitting in.

"Yeah, this is not what I thought it was going to be like," I said to myself as I took the retractable leash off of the dog. I went from anxious to excited to uncertain in the span of three hours. I decided to watch TV for the first time since having my glasses. Nothing was quite clear, but I was able to see and follow the sports news without much effort.

"At least I can watch TV, again," I said to myself. At that moment, a caption came on the screen. I wasn't able to make out what it said without moving much closer to the screen.

"I guess."

I found myself getting a bit frustrated. I was finding that it was much more of an adjustment than I had hoped. About that time, my phone chimed. Because I didn't have reading glasses yet, I still used the magnifying glass to read the small print. I opened my phone and I was able to make out that I had several unread texts. I used the expanding feature to enlarge the text messages. The uplifting texts were responses to the photo of my new frames that I sent earlier to my family and friends in the group text thread. I felt comforted by their words.

I sat and thought about everything I had been through. I had come a long way. And even though this adjustment would be more difficult than I had previously expected, I would have to reinforce in myself that there was more to come from this.

Look, Daniel. You still have a lot going on with your eyes. Hell, Schneider didn't think you'd see anything out of this eye. We're good. It will get better; it has to. Just give yourself a little more grace and time to adjust.

I spent the next hour exercising my eyes and looking at everything I hadn't been able to see. I found pictures and went through them, admiring and reminiscing on those moments. One was of Brandy and me in New Orleans. It had been nearly a year since that trip. I was now preparing to go on the most meaningful trip of our relationship.

I heard the garage open and Brandy's car pulling in. The dog always went nuts knowing she was home. I cracked the door and let Minx out to see her and I hid in the bathroom. I had yet to tell her I got my glasses.

"Daniel, my love?!" she called out as she entered through the door. I came from behind her and covered her eyes.

"This is how I felt the past seven months, and now…"

I took my hands off her eyes and turned her toward me. She let out a joyous yelp and grabbed my face. She smiled hard and gave me a kiss.

"They came! Oh, wow! You look so handsome!" She was so excited for me.

"How is your vision? Can you see this?" She began twerking and dancing, as if to entice me. I replied, "Oh my goodness! I'm healed!" We both laughed hysterically.

I described how my vision was and the obvious limitations I had, but because she was excited, I was, too. We both agreed that with more time, procedures, and healing that things would hopefully continue to improve.

"I am so proud of you for getting this far. For now, let's get ready for Minnesota!"

**

As concerned as I was before we left for Minnesota, I hardly thought about any of those things while we were there. I learned to survey my surroundings before moving to be sure I was able to navigate without running into anything or anyone. At times, I challenged myself to get around and find things in the hotel. Several members of Brandy's family went swimming, and I decided to stay back in the room. I hadn't been working out, so I didn't want to take off my shirt. After some thought, I got over myself and decided to find them. With some patience, attention to detail, and help from patrons I saw walking around in swimwear, I was able to locate them. Brandy was excited to see that I had made it on my own. We left the pool early to get upstairs and have some alone time before Blake and his cousins returned to the room. We stayed busy and had so much fun that I didn't think about my limitations. The more I wore my new glasses, the better I adjusted to them.

***

The magnifying reading glasses were shipped to my house while we were in Minnesota, and I was able to take them on my next trip. We only had a few days to be home before Brandy and I would leave for our trip to Panama City. It was a much-needed trip for both of us. We spent most of the time near the oceanfront and relaxing by the beach as the warm sun beamed down on us.

As we walked the beach one evening before dinner, I peered as far as I could toward the sun setting behind what seemed like a never-ending bed of water. The sun was evident, but I struggled to follow the watercrafts and birds as they flew high over the ocean. Instead of being happy that I had any vision, I began to grow agitated. Maybe I thought the glasses would work some type of magic and my vision would allow me to function normally. It had only been two weeks since I had my glasses, and I was doing things for myself that I hadn't been able to do in some time. I asked God to give me enough to be able to see my future wife, family, and friends. I told Him that I would make the best out of whatever He gave me. It seemed that He did just that, but at times I found myself less than grateful.

Chapter 35
Fake It 'Til You Make It

Every day began the same. I woke up to Brandy and Blake preparing to leave the house and start their day. I sat at the edge of the bed for a few minutes and let my sight adjust. Then I felt my way toward the medicine cabinets, where I took my slew of daily medications. From there, I helped prepare breakfast and pack their lunches. Brandy hugged and kissed me as they grabbed their things. I followed them to the garage door and wished them a good day.

"You too, Baby. I will call you on my break."

Once the garage door closed behind them, I was left with silence. For the next several hours, I would sit in the living room with the TV on, watching the walls. I'd find myself lost in thought, reliving the events that got me to this point. I would eventually make my way outside and have long talks with God and myself. I also talked to the dog, but she seemed to grow annoyed when I directed my words at her. Her annoyance was likely due to the fact I would elevate my voice the longer I talked.

My conversations would go from deep, to dark, and then intense. I found myself rehashing the moments that led up to my loss of sight, and what I'd do if I could have that time back. I discussed how past achievements and experiences shaped my life up to that point and how recent circumstances had derailed every plan I had laid out. I prayed often and vented even more often. I didn't know if these conversations did more harm than good. At times, it felt like I was remedying myself; other times it felt as if I was tormenting myself. I didn't want to express all this to my loved ones, but it was spilling over the more secluded and detached I became from normalcy. Since early on in my life, I managed the things that bothered me by simply avoiding dealing with them. It was my way of controlling the situation. But eventually, I had to face the truth. And like the saying goes, "the truth hurts." So, I became very good at putting on a smile, even when I felt I had nothing to smile about.

I knew I was growing deeply depressed, but as I had done many times in the past, I hid it. I was already embarrassed and afraid of anyone seeing me as I was. Not letting out my feelings just magnified things. With this being my everyday norm, time seemed to crawl and speed all at the same time.

***

"Hey Baby, we're home."

At times, they would arrive home and I could hear them, but I seemed to be paralyzed. I literally had to force myself out of idle, as if I were a computer program that got stuck and could not move on to the next process. Once I did gather myself, I'd quickly get into character.

"Good evening, baby. How was your day at work?"

I listened to her tales from co-workers who shared their personal stories with her. She was so animated that many times I painted the images of her words in my mind and imagined those instances as if I was actually there. My imagination became more vivid as my sight had become limited. I looked forward to her stories, even though I yearned to be able to share stories of my own.

"So how was your day, baby?" she would ask, hoping I would tell her something new.

"It was fine. Did a lot of talking to God and Minx. Just trying to stay positive. Other than that, I didn't do much of anything."

That was the best answer I could come up with, considering what the truth was. I knew if she could see me inside out, then she would be terrified. I wasn't holding it in for me; I was ready to explode. I was doing this for everyone in my corner. I was doing this to prove the doctors wrong. I was doing this for all the jokes, slights, and doubts ever aimed at me. Maybe it was selfish to hold back those emotions and pretend it was "all good," but I wasn't about to be weak in a time when so many had been strong for me. I was going to remain strong on the outside, even if I was going insane internally.

In an appointment with my therapist, I discussed this.

"So, it makes you feel empowered and in control when you can suppress those feelings. You're protecting others by holding back your feelings. Would you say that is accurate?" my therapist questioned me as I sat in the comfy red chair. "You seem to be in control of something again. You can show her how much you care for her by protecting her."

I didn't want to admit, but once again, he had judged my motivations correctly. I was indeed attempting to grasp ahold of whatever I could control in my life.

"Yes, but is that wrong? I mean, how much of myself do I have to give up in order to be normal? I mean, my defensive posture and desire to protect my family is normal, right?" He had me questioning everything I was doing. I started to feel bad for withholding so much from Brandy, my dad, my brothers, my friends, my family. Everyone.

"Daniel, it's not my place to tell you that it's wrong. I actually think you are incredibly strong to harbor so much. I ask you this: How much is holding on to that anger and sadness helping you?" My therapist paused to give me time to think about it. "To me, it seems as if you really want to share your feelings, but you need to feel safe. You don't want to be misjudged and you don't want to transfer that pain to your loved ones."

I interrupted him saying, "Yes, I don't want my pain to be confused. I don't want them to think it's about them. I don't want them to hurt because I hurt."

We both paused. I felt so uncomfortable expressing how it all made me feel. I had learned long ago how to hide feelings like this. In the past, when my emotions were unchecked, it had a ripple effect on those around me. If I got emotional, then my family and friends would get emotional along with me. I had an adverse impact on their state of mind, and it made me feel guilty that I influenced them in a negative way. So, I just tried to tuck those feelings away as best I could to protect my loved ones. But those feelings are always tough to conceal.

"Daniel, you cannot keep your family safe. They see you and know that you are hurting. They will hurt with you because they love you and want to help you deal with the hurt. If you keep trying to hide it from them and don't find a way to get it out, it will rear itself in an extremely ugly way."

We both sat in silence as I wrapped my mind around our discussion.

After a few moments, the therapist spoke again.

"I want you to stop thinking about everyone else for a second. Just think about yourself."

I focused my mind on myself as the man I was before everything happened.

"I want you to think about things you enjoyed doing. You were people-oriented and sociable. You were an athlete and loved fitness. We've talked about your music and production background. Think about those things that made you feel normal."

I imagined leaving the gym and heading out on the town to enjoy myself. I saw myself driving with the top down as the city lights streaked across my skin. I turned the music up and closed my eyes as I sped up the highway.

"You should try to incorporate these things back in your life in some way. Just think about the things you've enjoyed and used to express yourself in the past. I really think you should be doing those things, even if you choose not to share them with anyone. Use these things as your canvas. I encourage expressing your thoughts and feelings, however they come out. I believe it will help you and you never know who else it could help."

It was time to reimagine what my life would look like going forward. I couldn't hold on to the exact same dreams and plans I had before I lost my sight. Even if I was able to accomplish those things, I had to be willing to accept that I would have to take additional steps or a new approach to get them.

"Let's schedule our next appointment for next week," my therapist said. "Your story is unique. Life may forever be different for you, but you have what it takes to overcome and be better because of it. Overcoming adversity is everyone's favorite story."

I nodded and set my next appointment before we headed out of the room.

He guided me to the waiting area where my father was sitting. As we rode home in silence, I recalled my conversations with my therapist. I thought about what I would say if I did start writing. I pondered on how I could chronicle my thoughts and express myself creatively. Though my reading glasses allowed me to see and read, it would take a lot of time to write all I had on my heart.

"Open Voice Recorder," I stated to the voice command on my phone. My father looked at me and asked, "Do you need me to help?"

I had left my reading glasses at home and couldn't make out the small print on my phone. I could have just waited until I got home, but I had waited on the things that meant most to me long enough.

"Here, just find my Voice Recorder," I said to my dad. He opened the application and guided my finger to where the record icon was on the screen.

"The record button is here, in the middle toward the bottom," he pointed out to me. I smiled and closed the application.

I arrived home and grabbed my reading glasses before heading to the bathroom. I closed the toilet lid and sat there for a few hours recording myself on Voice Recorder and video. I didn't have anything in particular to say. I just vented and expressed my feelings. Because I knew I wouldn't be met with any opposition, I said a lot of things that I was reluctant to say to my therapist or anyone else, but I needed to get it out. I was losing faith, and I felt like I would be better off dead than to live with all these feelings bottled up inside.

I eventually got up from the restroom and ended up on the couch. Staring at the ceiling, I pondered the future and what it truly had in store. I had taken on the responsibility of providing a life for a family.

How am I going to get out of this hole and take care of them? I thought.

I must have thought so hard that I tired myself out. I remember coming to and hearing Brandy in the kitchen, telling Blake to take Minx for a walk. With those thoughts still on my mind, I quickly grew sad. My health was not my main concern. The beautiful woman in the kitchen and how I was going to provide for her was. She turned the corner as I sat up to greet her.

"Hey, future husband. How was your day?"

I forced myself to smile, though I was far from happy.

Chapter 36
Same Crap Different Toilet

Summer concluded, as did any excitement I had for the vision I had regained. I thought that more time wearing my frames would yield better clarity, but it became apparent that my eyes were long from being fixed. And so was my pride. Fall came swiftly, the weather cooled and leaves began to accumulate on the ground.

I had 10 doctor appointments in the month of October:

My Aunt Maychelle took me to my retina surgeon, Dr. Schneider, who was really impressed that my vision had improved to 20/90, but still scheduled another surgery to remove more scarring from my retina. She also took me to see a podiatrist.

My dad took me to a diabetes check-up with my primary care physician and to the chiropractor. I had read that depression is linked to poor posture, back pain, and muscle deterioration, and I was experiencing pain in my back. Darrell took me to the Sarah Cannon Cancer Research Center to meet with the lead oncologist, who simply reiterated how Chronic Myeloid Leukemia can obstruct blood flow and strain the blood vessels in my body.

As much as I hated going to all the appointments, I knew it was a must. If not for me, then I at least wanted to do it for them. They were the ones keeping me going when I didn't have the desire to do it for myself.

I felt comfort when they were with me, but each time they left me at home, and closed the door behind them, I was alone with my feelings. I felt overwhelmed by sadness, fury, and extreme guilt. I grew far too familiar with these feelings – more than I ever liked to admit.

I deliberately missed my last scheduled appointment with my therapist because I no longer wanted to talk about my issues to anyone. Instead, I recorded several voice and video entries on my phone. Almost all of the entries captured the resentment and unrest I felt from my loss of independence. I wasn't cleared to go to the gym, I was advised not to be out alone in case I had an emergency, and I had no way to get out of the home without someone picking me up. The walls of our home seemed to be slowly closing in on me and leaving me less space and optimism. The light at the end of the tunnel that I'd hope for seemed to be further out of my reach.

I spent so much time in the living room that my mind began playing tricks on me, and strange things seemed to keep happening. At times, our closet door opened on its own. Shadows on the floor moved from one area of the room to the windows, and then disappeared into the sunlight. The blinds in the backdoor window moved as if someone brushed them as they walked by every afternoon. Sitting in the same spot every day wasn't working for me. So, I decided to move my daily pity party to the bonus room, a sparsely used upstairs area of the house. It was a new place in our home to isolate my isolation. But, even with a new location, I could still hear the ruffling blinds every afternoon. I never kept up with the time, but the ruffling never took a day off, at least not during the work week. Maybe it was the HVAC system cycling on and off that caused the air to circulate and rustle the blinds. I could never figure it out. Oddly enough, it didn't scare me, even after experiencing this time and time again. Instead, I greeted it with apathy and sarcasm.

"There you go, again, with your bitch-ass. I know I'm blind. I don't need another reminder. Blinds. Blind. I get it. Shut the fuck up!" I said with an elevated voice.

A fly on the wall might have said that I was becoming unhinged. My outbursts became more frequent, as I constantly suppressed my true feelings. Recording my thoughts on my phone gave me an outlet, but I felt as alone as ever. Talking to friends and family no longer gave me the boost it offered in the beginning. I didn't want to hear, "God has a plan for you. God is with you. It's going to be fine."

In September, as Brandy and I took our engagement pictures at the Bicentennial Mall amphitheater, an older lady complimented us.

"How beautiful. God is good, ain't He?!" The traditional response to the saying is to reply, "All the time!" Instead, I said under my breath, "I guess."

My love for Brandy was not to be confused with my disappointment, though. I just didn't know how to have faith in Him any longer. I'd find myself unengaged, standing during prayer at church with my eyes open. I didn't see the point of praying for myself. God had already planned my life, and I was in this position because this is what He wanted. Right?

I took care of myself enough to avoid these kinds of issues with diabetes, I thought. So, why would God allow diabetes and leukemia, to attack my life? How does a condition that I have managed my whole life get confused with complications from a disease I never knew I had? I feel I deserve better than this.

I felt like God made a mistake, and I was not ready to accept his plan for my life. I had become withdrawn, stuck in idle. I reminisced on better times, such as college, early adulthood, and all the things I did and I regretted not doing. Though I grew resentful, I couldn't allow my disappointment to keep me from taking care of my health concerns. If I was going to be a husband and father figure, I would have to remain steadfast on rehabilitating my body as best I could.

I needed to take a hard look at myself and what path I was headed down. I once attended church and listened to my brother, Darrell, preach a sermon about overcoming grief. He admitted that he had been upset with God for our mother's passing. He expressed making certain decisions that were counterproductive of him overcoming this grief and that he had to learn to forgive God and himself. It was as if he was speaking for me, also. I couldn't figure out how to verbalize my feelings, but Darrell said it better than I could have ever done. In order for me to continue to have a relationship with God, I first had to learn to be okay with the decisions that were being made about my life and accept the things that God allowed to happen such as letting my mom die. I had to forgive myself for not knowing how to deal with her death or even recognize that she was sick.

On one of my visits to Tennessee Retina, I met an older lady while sitting in the main waiting room. She sat nearby and talked to me about losing her sight in one eye and what to look forward to when I got to be her age. Little did she know I was already dealing with more than she could have imagined. She asked me about my situation and we started a pleasant conversation. As I started to express my hurt and how I questioned God's choice to place this burden on me, she quickly interrupted me.

"Son, don't you question God," she admonished me. "He is all-seeing and all-knowing! He knows what's best. He placed this on you, but maybe it shielded you from what could have happened. Instead of being bitter, you should thank God, because life is tough. But it is precious and as long as you have breath, you have the ability to do anything. Feeling sorry for yourself ain't fixing nothing."

Before she could finish her response, the technician called her name to see her doctor. She stood from her seat, turned to me and said, "When you start to raise your voice to God, remember that everything happens for a reason. Believe that, because life don't owe you nothing."

She turned and walked away. I couldn't believe she actually said that. I felt like she discounted how I felt. What if the shoe was on the other foot? I regretted even getting deep into a discussion with her. I lifted my head to watch her smudged image exit the room. I looked away from her, began staring at the floor in a trance-like state and responded under my breath, "Man… fuck you." I didn't know if the other patients in the waiting room heard me curse at the older lady, but I was not even in a mental state that would allow me to be embarrassed by my behavior. I was furious at more than just her admonishments. I was angry, and it was beginning to consume me.

The visit with my doctor that day didn't make things any better. During my appointment, Dr. Schneider scheduled another surgery for October 15 to remove scar tissue. I called Brandy. She was happy because she said the surgery was evidence that healing was happening, but I wasn't nearly as optimistic. And I proceeded to vent.

"I watched my food intake, I worked out, I went to work, and I wasn't a bad person to others. What am I supposed to be optimistic about?" I couldn't hold it in any longer.

Brandy was bothered by my words and replied, "Daniel, I know you feel like you did enough to stay healthy and avoid this, but did you check your sugar like you should have? Did you go to your scheduled diabetes checkups? Did you listen to your body when you started to feel sluggish? If you can't answer yes to those questions, then maybe you could have done more. You can't go back. So, you have to deal with this head on."

As true as her words were, they left me annoyed, so much that I rejected everything else she had to say. I wanted to reply, but instead I sat unengaged as she continued.

"There are many people who don't take care of themselves, and they seem to just skate by. Unfortunately, you had some issues that were unforeseen. I am here all the way, baby. It might not be fair, but we are here," she said. I had nothing more to say or offer, so we ended the conversation.

Not only was I annoyed by the fact that I had to undergo another surgery, but I was also vexed by Brandy's reply. I know she wanted nothing more than to see me overcome this, but there was nothing she could do to make me feel better about my circumstances. I felt alone in this journey at times, but it was because I refrained from sharing my pain, and I refused to let others all the way in. I felt like I was running on a treadmill, working to alleviate myself of these circumstances, but stuck in the same place. My situation never seemed to change, no matter how patient I was.

I was in such a bad mood the remainder of the day that I purposely sat on the couch; in the same spot I had grown so familiar with in the past several months. I lay there with the dog keeping me company, looking at the ceiling asking God, the Devil, and the universe, What's next, huh? What you got for me next?

Chapter 37
Sunken Place

My mental health was unraveling fast. I didn't want to talk much about it, so one day when my primary care physician asked how I was doing, I gave her my rehearsed response that I gave everyone when I didn't want to disclose my true emotions.

"Just taking it day by day. Trying to remain hopeful and waiting on God."

I had said it so often, but on that day, I caught myself. I realized how untrue that was. Before I could finish my thought, Dr. Wolfe replied, "Well, I hope you continue to make progress. I believe you will, but don't be afraid to ask for help. Continue to make your appointments and take all your meds, including the antidepressant. I will get these prescriptions sent in. You come back in three months and let me know if you need anything."

I had stopped taking the antidepressant that Dr. Wolfe prescribed for me a few weeks earlier. It didn't help much. But that's probably because I was sabotaging the therapy. I was purposefully angry, upset and downtrodden. I'm sure the pills could've helped in some ways, but I didn't see the point in continuing because anybody who doesn't want to have hope won't find hope in a drug. If I didn't want to feel good about my situation, I wasn't going to feel good about it. I wasn't happy about where I was or about the incremental steps that I was making. I thought that I shouldn't be in this situation at all and things were not materializing at the pace that I thought they should. No matter what form or therapy I chose, it was going to be hard to fix my mental state because I wasn't ready to change. I was still in denial that I was even in my situation. When I couldn't face the truth, I tried to hide from it instead of meeting it head-on.

As Dr. Wolfe left the room, I sat there for a minute pondering how I had begun to slight God. I had been mad at God in my past, but never had the nerve to discredit Him. I was close to losing all hope that there would be any other significant improvements to my sight. The door closed behind her, and I gathered my backpack. With the thought still on my mind, I turned to walk out the door thinking,

I really don't care how God feels.

I was more down and disappointed than I had been since this journey had begun. The physical challenges with my vision, chronic myeloid leukemia, and diabetes were hard enough. But the mental turmoil and spiritual battles were just as vicious. My heart was growing heavier and heavier. I tried as best I could to smile, but sadness wore me like an ugly Christmas sweater in August.

After arriving home from the doctor's office, I made a strong alcoholic beverage, grabbed my phone, and made my way to the garage. I grabbed a chair, set the phone up on a shelf, and hit record on the video button. I took a long sip of my drink.

"I don't know how to express how tough this is. Life has been tough, even before all of this. I haven't had a hard life, but traveled down the rocky road. All this has made me stronger, but this shit here? Seeing how tough this is on my family is the hardest thing I have ever witnessed," I said to the phone as it recorded. I paused and sat thinking for a moment.

I thought about how I had witnessed my brothers in emotional turmoil over me. My closest friends all had struggled to accept that I was forever changed. I thought about my family members praying and crying for God to restore my health. And then, Brandy. I thought about our whirlwind relationship and how much fun and love we shared, but now I felt like a burden to her.

Pure rage ensued.

"Forget this shit. Yeah, I said it! What You gonna do, huh?! Take away my health?! Take my life?! You have already done that! What else You gonna do?! You know what You gonna do?! Not a damn thing, because You too busy doing nothing, while the Devil has his way! Rappers out here talking about, 'God blessing all the trap niggas.' Really? You can't be serious! How about You bless someone who believes in You? Bless someone who has tried to be a good person, both inside and out! Me! Bless me!"

I wasn't like Job in the Bible. When facing incredible adversity, his wife told him to "curse God and die." But Job restrained himself, and didn't sin. He held his tongue. I, in fact, cursed God. My tirade went on for several minutes. I screamed obscenities toward the heavens, as if God was hard of hearing. I knocked over items and hurled a nearby candle that was in a glass container to the ground with so much force that the shattered pieces dug into my legs as they ricocheted from the garage floor. I was not oblivious to the words coming from my mouth. I meant everything I said.

I knew I was wrong, but in the moment, I didn't care. No amount of therapy, encouraging words or prayers were going to fix me. I was in a downward spiral and didn't have the strength or the desire to pull up.

All of the pain and disappointment I had ever felt in my life erupted in an uncontrolled moment; from the loss of my mom to my stalled athletic career. The only person who would normally be able to calm me down – my mom – was gone. She was taken away from me. That pain is forever, and I never healed on the inside.

Now, my sight was being taken away. I felt like I couldn't catch a break, and it felt like He was steady taking jabs and blows at me.

Chapter 38
Me, Myself, and Eye

With everything that I had going on health-wise, I neglected the fact that I was supposed to be helping my fiancé plan a wedding. It wasn't on purpose, but I could be condescending and antagonistic towards many of the things that had been important to me and my soon-to-be wife.

We discussed scaling down the number of guests that were invited to the wedding to cut costs. We agreed to keep the list at 250 people, which seemed like a lot, but with the size of our families and friend circle that meant making some difficult decisions. I tried not to be bothered about eliminating invitees, so I hid my frustration. But it always came down to money.

"Brandy, I know you want to have a wedding videographer but I feel like it's too much money. And how many times are we actually going to watch it?" I argued.

"Daniel, you used to film weddings, so you should know the importance of having that keepsake," Brandy countered.

While I brought up several concerns, I was only looking at cost.

"The wedding is important to me. The video is not," I replied. "If it's that important to you, I can get Toney to do our wedding videography. He will give us a deal."

She seemed a little annoyed at my suggestion. Toney was my cousin and a skilled videographer. Using him to film the wedding wasn't the issue. She didn't appreciate my tone toward her idea.

"First, Toney is invited to the wedding, so shouldn't he be enjoying himself instead of working? Second, I don't know why you are even doing all of this. No offense to you or Toney, but we don't have a lot of time to make a decision. The wedding is in April, and while that may seem far off, we need to make these decisions now. Plus, I already talked to this company and I'm paying for this, not you. I really want this guy so that's what I'm doing."

Because money was short on my end, I was offended by her comment. While it was true that she had more money to spend towards the wedding, I wasn't trying to hear that. Though I paid my share of bills, pay from long-term disability benefits was certainly short of my normal salary. Not to mention, I couldn't do any of my side hustles, which really hurt my pockets.

I got up and left the room. She tried to continue the conversation upstairs, but I didn't say another word. I don't believe we spoke until she got home from work the following day.

***

Not having a job or a daily routine to keep me busy was becoming a big problem.

I always looked forward to football season and found myself trying to escape reality through sports more than ever. From constantly watching sports news to playing fantasy football and placing bets on games through online sports books, I found myself focusing on these things. But it was like trying to put a Band-Aid on a knife wound. No matter how much time I spent trying to distract myself, my reality was waiting on me at the door.

I continued to document my feelings through video and voice recordings, but I knew I needed something more because I wasn't actually working through any of my issues. I recalled the last appointment I had with my therapist and how he encouraged me to delve back into the hobbies that brought me joy. I pulled out my laptop in hopes that I could see the small print enough to pull up my music production program.

As I peered at the screen with my magnifying reading glasses, it quickly became apparent that I would not be able to function like this. My neck ached as I leaned closer to the screen, and I got headaches switching back and forth from my reading glasses to my distance glasses. It took me ten minutes just to get the program up. Once I was able to launch the application, I ran into even more issues adjusting the settings to see the screen clearly. I always found a way to work through problems, but after nearly an hour of fighting to adjust the settings, I gave up.

I decided to go out to my car, which had been parked on Brandy's driveway since I'd first gone blind. Inside the CD player, which I barely used when I did drive, was a CD of several tracks I had made in the past. I retreated back inside to the bonus room and put the CD in my laptop. I plugged up my speaker system and played the first track. As I listened to the tracks, I began to think about the positive experiences I had writing and producing music. I listened to those tracks for hours. My excitement grew with each track that played, as if it were the first time I had heard them.

Music and writing had always given me an outlet and a way to connect with others. They were a way of self-expression. As a baritone player in middle school, I led my band classmates in playing popular songs in our concerts. I considered singing in ensemble and the church choir in high school. Decosta, David, Theo, and I, along with a host of our friends, all hoped to accomplish our music writing and production goals. I participated in numerous producer competitions and was even offered a publishing contract with a local producer who had some mainstream successes. My childhood friend, Brian Baker, helped me come up with my producer name; Drum-Right. In college and early adulthood, producing became an identity for me when I was trying to discover who I truly was. I really enjoyed music production, writing poems, songs, short stories, and even acting. Although my career ultimately went in a different direction, I always found time to indulge in these leisure activities.

***

Another way I tried to pass the time each day was by reconnecting with friends and family. I had become disconnected and dejected. Watching television was not my idea of liberation. I needed to be a part of life outside of the familiar walls of our bonus room, and I needed it to be on my terms. Though I was still uncomfortable out in public, I was grateful to have friends and family who could spend some time with me. I told myself I would make an effort to get out of the house some. I called my cousin Ryan, with whom I shared a close bond. He was free and came over the same day I called.

"Hey, cuz. I'm outside," he called to say.

I opened the garage and let him in. He gave me a big hug, as he always did when he saw me. We sat on the back patio and talked for a while about life. We were both ambitious and had a lot of business plans and dreams that we wanted to accomplish, but we both had a multitude of hindrances we encountered along the way. His mother passed away the same year as mine, so that's one journey we traveled together.

"Hey cuz, this ain't no different. You need anything, I got you. Or at least I will try," he said as he sipped his beverage and puffed on a cigar.

"I know y'all doing a lot of things out here and I'm sure y'all are having a blast. Just be careful out here. Avoid the mess and keep good people close. Hopefully, I'll be able to get back out here with y'all one day," I said as we finished up our conversation and left for the gas station up the street. As we pulled up, I unbuckled my seat belt and opened my door. I asked Ryan if he wanted anything from inside.

"Do you need me to go in with you, cuz?" he asked before I got out of the car. My pride wouldn't allow me to accept his help. Plus, I had been in the store by myself a few times before, so I wasn't concerned. I'd just take my time if I had any difficulty getting around by myself.

"I'll be fine," I said as I unfastened my seatbelt.

I exited the car and made my way toward the building. Ryan had parked at the vacuum and air pump, so I had a longer walk than usual. As I got out of the car, I thought about how much I missed being able to just run down the street if I wanted. I thought to myself, If only I could see enough to ride my bike.

I walked aimlessly while in mid-thought and heard my cousin's voice call out to me.

"Cuz! Cuz!"

The urgency in his voice suggested that maybe I had forgotten something in the car that I needed in the store. I patted my pocket to make sure I had my wallet. Before I knew it, Ryan had run to catch up with me and was right by my side.

"Cuz, you walking in the wrong direction! I was like, 'where's he going?'" he said trying not to laugh too hard. I chuckled thinking how silly I looked walking toward the fast-food restaurant which was several feet away from the gas station.

As I made my way in the correct direction, I began to feel a little embarrassed. I walked around the gas station wondering who else was watching as Ryan called my name from across the parking lot. It was hard not to feel insecure. I didn't want to live a life where my disabilities were obvious and exposed, but each new experience caused me to doubt myself a little bit more.

Ryan dropped me back off at the house as he headed out for the evening.

"Hey cuz, don't sweat that," he said trying to encourage me. I'm sure he knew I was embarrassed, but I played it off as if it wasn't a big deal to me. I went inside to sit in the bonus room and listened to my tracks, but I wasn't able to take that moment off my mind.

***

On another occasion, a close childhood friend who I hadn't heard from since I had been sick reached out to me to hang out.

"Bro, I'm going to come pick you up, and we can just go kick it. We can go grab something to eat and just catch up."

We decided to get together on the following Tuesday afternoon, but when Tuesday came, I heard nothing from him. I didn't assume anything, but I just counted it as he got caught up. I knew I needed to keep myself busy so that I wouldn't dwell on negativity, so I turned back to my music. Instead of hanging out and catching up with my old friend, I got my laptop out and tried to get my music production software going.

My stubbornness had proved on many occasions to be a repetitive stumbling block. I believed in myself and my way so much at times that I'd miss opportunities to fix an issue more efficiently. This was the case with visual settings on my laptop. I knew I could hook up the computer to my 55-inch flat screen TV, but I needed the correct adapter. I purchased an adapter that I was sure would get me going. Unfortunately, I ordered the same piece from two different vendors and neither of them worked. I finally looked up components to my laptop model and purchased the correct item; a mini display port adapter. The order confirmation stated it would take three to five business days to arrive. After ordering the wrong part twice, what was another three to five days?

While waiting on the correct adapter to arrive, my phone rang.

There was no name that popped up on the screen, so I put my reading glasses on to view the number. The number looked familiar, so I answered.

"Bro, what's good? Man, my bad I did not mean to leave you out there like that," my buddy who stood me up the week before said to me. He really didn't give me an excuse, but he wanted to reschedule.

"Bro, I don't have nothing but time. How about we shoot for Monday? I'll just be home with the dog so that would be a perfect time to get out and kick it."

He agreed and told me that he would be over at 1:00 p.m. the following Monday.

***

We went to church on Sunday, and I was met with hugs and encouragement by several members of the congregation. It was always appreciated that people come and show me love, but I also encountered feelings I had desperately tried to avoid. Feeling needy and helpless tanked my spirit. And then, the word "disabled" was finally spoken.

A family friend introduced me to a church member who she thought could help me.

"She's an occupational therapist and treats a lot of disabled people. She is also a personal trainer. She can work with you and get you back in great shape. I'm going to tell her all about you and have her contact you on Facebook," she said.

While I knew my friend meant no harm, I was offended by several things she suggested.

Her audacity to assume that I needed assistance doing anything, especially losing weight, annoyed me so much that I mentally blocked out the rest of her commentary. What I couldn't forget was that she referred to me as disabled.

That word was a shock to my system because I never wanted to be labeled. And even though, I was technically already receiving "disability" benefits from the government, the idea of being perceived by others as incapable and incomplete hurt my feelings. There was something about hearing people refer to me in a way that was inconsistent with how I viewed myself that didn't sit well with me.

And honestly, it scared me. I feared being dependent. I always had problems asking for help. It was a natural part of my personality. I never wanted anyone to have a reason to pity me or dismiss me as irrelevant. Ironically, when I worked in the Mayor's Office, I never considered that the people who were calling each day to get assistance might have possessed these same feelings. Now, I was finding myself in a position where I, too, was vulnerable and needed to rely on others just to make it through the day.

I wasn't detached from reality. I understood that people throughout history had changed the world after losing their sight. Famed musician Ray Charles became blind as a child after suffering from juvenile glaucoma. Helen

Keller, a renowned author and activist, was less than two years old before a severe illness robbed her of vision. And Italian tenor Andrea Bocelli who sold over 65 million albums worldwide completely lost his sight after a sports injury. The list of blind changemakers – famous ones and everyday people – could go on for days. It just never occurred to me that I might one day have to navigate life without sight. I was being forced to view myself in a different way.

I wanted to see well enough to get around on my own and thought I could. The thought of forever needing assistance to do even the simplest things, was terrifying. I couldn't get it off my mind the rest of the day, which certainly ruined the remainder of my weekend.

***

After getting my clothes together for the rescheduled afternoon outing with my homeboy, I sat around and listened to the audiobook of Tim Tebow's Through My Eyes which was published in 2013. My vocational rehabilitation program was in partnership with The National Library Service for the Blind and Print Disabled, Library of Congress, and they sent me the book on an audio cartridge. He spoke about different trials in his upbringing and how God worked in those situations to give him the opportunity to prove himself. I began thinking about my own circumstances and whether God would allow me to use my situations to do the same. Before I knew it, 11:45 a.m. had come around. I headed upstairs to take a shower and chill before my buddy arrived.

"I'm not about to let this man get me again. I'll call him right at 12:30 p.m. to see where he's at," I said joking to myself in the mirror. I even sent him a courtesy reminder via text message.

"Let me know when you are outside and I will come out to you."

Thirty minutes went by and I didn't hear from him. I didn't jump to any conclusions, as he had a master's degree in being late. I turned on sports news and watched the pregame show for the upcoming football game that night. As I viewed the program, I kept a mental note of how much time I thought had gone by. Segment after segment started and ended. I kept up with every commercial break. I made sure my ringer volume was on its highest setting. I even restarted my phone to be sure that I hadn't lost signal.

Okay. 1:40 p.m.

By this time, I began having negative thoughts. I thought about how I had visited him when he was locked up for pretty stiff charges. I, also, thought about how I helped him take care of some personal matters while he was incarcerated. I knew he had a lot going on and was trying to get on his feet, but I couldn't understand why he wouldn't call. I didn't want to think he didn't care enough about what I was going through, but it felt that way.

Wow! It's like that?!

I was disappointed and hurt more than anything. With the countless days and hours I spent at home alone, I was having second thoughts about even considering stepping out. All I wanted was to feel normal. All I wanted was to be normal. As I sat and thought about my friend not showing up, frustration filled my thoughts.

Not even a call? After all we've been through. How do you make plans to see your sick friend and just decide to disappear? Won't be a third time!

As I continued to scold my old friend, the doorbell rang. My attitude quickly changed as I scurried toward the door. I immediately began to feel a little bad about how hard I had criticized him, even though I knew he couldn't hear those things being said.

I fixed my shirt as I reach for the door handle. I pulled the door open quickly and looked out the storm door as well as I could. The sun was coming in at an angle and caught my left eye. I blocked the sun with my hand and looked again. No one was there. It left me extremely confused.

Did I not just hear the doorbell ring?

At that moment, I heard the door of a delivery truck close. I stretched my neck out watching as best I could as the driver got back in the cabin and drove away. I looked down to see a package on the welcome mat. I didn't even care to pick the package up. I closed the storm door and walked back to the couch. I sat down and put my head in my hands. It hurt that my friend stood me up. But, it really hurt that the only option I had was to be stood up. I would normally move on and find something better to do, but now I didn't have that option.

I sat sulking for at least an hour before I got up to close the front door. I looked outside and remembered the package still sitting on the welcome mat. I opened the storm door to pick it up and put on my readers. The package was for me. Inside the crayon-box-sized package was an even smaller package. I opened it. It was the mini display port adapter for my laptop. I immediately headed inside to hook it up.

Chapter 39
Hard Conversations

I didn't have a legit setup for my music equipment at my new home with Brandy and Blake, considering I hadn't done anything music related in some time. I stored my keyboard and equipment on an old air hockey table that Blake had in the bonus room. There was an old analog television that used audio/visual cables, but it was useless because it was not HDMI compatible. Blake had a flat screen TV in his room, but I didn't want to keep moving it back and forth. I went downstairs and took a rolling cart that we used for storing drinks. I wheeled it into the living room and I set up my equipment there.

The cart was stomach height, which was perfect. I connected the adapter and HDMI cord from our living room TV to my laptop. I powered on the TV and put on my reading glasses to look up connectivity directions on my phone. Before I could finish the second sentence, I looked up and noticed my computer screen on the 55-inch TV. I spent the next hour installing updates on my computer. While the updates completed, I pulled up my music streaming subscription on my phone and played the most current hip hop playlist. I was delighted by the anticipation, listening to song after song. The sense of normalcy this brought was more than welcomed. I didn't get to work on any music before Brandy and Blake came in to see me in the living room with cords and plugs going in multiple directions.

"Hey Baby! I thought you'd be gone to hang out with your friend. How was your day?" Brandy asked as she came around the corner. She saw me standing there in front of the TV with music playing. For a moment I was afraid she would be upset to see the living room in such disarray.

"Well, look at you," she said proudly. I smiled and turned back toward the TV.

"I hope you're not planning on leaving that there forever, though," she said jokingly as she walked back in the kitchen.

Blake had heard about my music background, but this was his first time seeing my equipment hooked up. He was very intrigued. I pulled up the editing software as the updates finished and synced a piano plug-in to my keyboard. We played around for about an hour before dinner.

"Man, Daniel! We make beats on the table during lunch and the cafeteria monitors get mad at us," Blake said.

I laughed at him and asked, "They still do that?"

I told Blake that he could come in and play on the piano whenever he wanted. I showed him how to start up the program and how to send the sound to the keyboard. With everything that I had going, I didn't recognize I had not engaged Blake as much as I had previously. His father was in his life and I never felt like I had to make up for that, but I knew I would have an important role going forward. I had allowed my illnesses and misfortune to cause me to neglect that responsibility. His interest in making music got me excited and I gladly offered to introduce him to that.

Instead of joining Brandy after dinner in our bedroom, I sat downstairs finishing up the final task on my computer. My mood always influenced what music I listened to and made. I began thinking about the music from a commercial for a 2015 pickup truck. The piano melody that played was deep, moving, and full of emotion. It surprised me to hear that it was the music from a truck commercial. That music spoke to me. I did an online search for the commercial to find the song that I had played over and over in my head. A video came up with the commercial almost immediately. It was the first time I actually saw the commercial. As I listened to the music, I got chills. It took me back to those trying times earlier in the year. Memories of helplessness and confinement. My eyes watered as those moments flooded my memory. I grabbed Brandy's tablet and opened an app that identified the song title and artist. I quickly found a site to download the original song, and I played the song on repeat as I began to write. The words poured out of me and began to fill the page. I wrote and rehearsed several lines before I got to a point where the words became harder to put together and my mind became cluttered. Brandy eventually called down to me and suggested I come to bed.

As I lay there that night, I couldn't help but hold Brandy. Her presence eased me, though I had so much running through my mind. I eventually grew tired and readied myself to go to sleep. I fell asleep with so much on my mind that it bled over into my subconscious and gave me nightmares. I dreamed of chaos all around me, but instead of it being intimidating and intolerable, I was unfazed. From constant doctor visits and surgeries to my envy of others who were in a much better place than I was, it all manifested itself in my subconscious. I startled as I awoke, and Brandy wrapped her arm around me.

"Are you okay?" she asked. I nodded and sat at the edge of the bed feeling drained and unrested.

"Yeah, yeah," I uttered as I sat up trying not to disturb Brandy and the dog any longer. Though my dreams were full of detail, the feeling was extremely abstract. I had no answers as to why or how I was supposed to make sense of my new normal. Since losing my sight, my dreams were often haunting and exhausting.

Bad dreams and lack of sleep compounded things, and mentally I couldn't ignore where I was. The hard conversations that resulted with others, myself, God, and anything else listening was a vent, but the dreams were different. In my dreams, it was like I could see everything, but see nothing all at the same time. I couldn't get back settled, so I sat in the bed and wrote.

Night turned into day, and Brandy eventually awoke and got herself together to start her day. I quickly jotted down the thoughts that stuck out from my dream before helping Brandy gather her things and exit for work. After she left, I sat back down to write and go over my writings from the night before, but couldn't find the words to express myself. The writings expressed my thoughts and questioned why I was in this living hell, compared to the life that I had planned for myself, but I could not find answers or gain clarity.

Instead of getting frustrated, I put the pen and paper to the side, closed my text application on my phone, and began working on turning the sample I wanted to use into a track. I hadn't worked on anything since getting my computer back up and running, so finding the sample that had been in my head for so long gave me plenty of motivation. I began looking for drum sounds in my music editing program.

Snares, claps, hi hats, and kick drums were all aligned in the editing window. I always started off my tracks with creating the drum pattern I heard in my head. Once I got a general loop going, I focused on chopping the sample up for the melody. I found a very clear and defined point in the sample and trimmed the track to create a repetitive loop. I saved that small sampled area and imported it into the editing window. The sample was far too slow initially. I used a tempo mapping tool to adjust the speed of the sample. I matched the tempo perfectly with the drum pattern. I listened to the beginning draft of the track. It was still raw and unfinished, but I was nearing that sweet spot where the beat had a personality. I just couldn't figure out what was missing.

I laid a general baseline and made an 8-bar loop. It needed something ambient, but filling. It needed to be distinct, but not take away from the melody or dark energy that I was seeking. I searched through my background noise and effects folders but found nothing that fit. Instead of forcing it, I took a break and went to the kitchen to fix a snack. I prepared a cup of coffee and before I could add cream and sweetener, I heard a thunder clap on the TV.

"That's it!" I said to myself smiling as I had found the missing ambience I was searching for.

I rushed back into the living room and turned the TV screen back to the input that my computer was set up on. I quickly began searching through outdoor and nature sound effects. Not long into my search, I found the perfect set of thunder claps and lightning strikes to add. I inserted them at specific places to compliment the music. It was perfect. I let the sample play for several minutes as I vibed to the beat. The energy and tempo of the drafted track moved me, both mentally and emotionally. The intensity of the music put me in a zone, and my anger and frustration came out through my lyrics.

Being creative gave me the ability to be raw and uncut. It was the true and appropriate vent that allowed me to tap into those feelings and not lie to myself. And I didn't have to rely on anyone else to do this. My friends couldn't let me down by standing me up. No one could take this away from me. My therapist was right. This was the perfect escape from my reality.

My heart raced as I repeated the lines to the music. Other thoughts and words started coming out from nowhere. I truly questioned the authenticity of being "blessed" in the previous 10 months. Those emotions began to spill out in my actions and words. Before I knew it, I had pushed the couch and coffee table so far forward that it almost knocked over my computer and keyboard. I paced as I continued to play the loop, seeing myself in the dream I had the night before. I began to tremble with anger. All that negative energy and those dark thoughts were coming out. My heart was pounding so hard, it felt as if it would rip right through my chest.

"God, what am I supposed to do?!" I yelled as hard as I could while standing up and looking at the ceiling. Tiny paws scurried up the steps, as I frightened Minx. I sat and began thinking about all the wrong I had done in my past. Those wrongs had me questioning whether karma had caught up with me. Yes, I can wrap my mind around the idea that diabetes causes retinopathy. But leukemia, too?! I felt like I was being served a double dose of bullshit. I put my face in my hands, and it all started pouring out.

This was a spiritual breaking point for me. All the emotions that I had been harboring began to violently spill out of me, similar to the way a science project bubbles over when baking soda and vinegar are mixed in a glass beaker. I was trying to embrace my emotions, but I still didn't accept my condition. So it became an internal battle of anger, lack of hope, and unwillingness to move forward. I was sorry for being angry, but still unable to get over myself. I was still in my pity party that I wasn't quite ready to leave.

"I'm sorry. I have been reckless with my words, and I am so sorry. Please take it away, God. Just give me back the life I had. I won't complain about anything ever again," I cried out, hoping that I had been having the longest nightmare in my life.

Chapter 40
When My Faith Grew Weak

On October 26th, I reported to the hospital for a scheduled biopsy. My oncologist wanted to check the DNA in my bone marrow for a chromosome defect associated with chronic myeloid leukemia. My white blood cell count and platelet levels had remained in normal range for quite some time. And my oncologist was impressed with my progress. The thought of leukemia was more of an inconvenience than a big concern for me. I knew that it was serious and if untreated could cost me my life, but my blood continued to yield positive results. The only issue I had with it was the medication, as it continued to make me ill.

The morning of my biopsy, my Aunt Maychelle took me to Southern Hills Hospital where my Aunt Tina awaited our arrival. She was the chaplain there. We greeted each other and talked about how life had been and what it had in store for me.

When my faith grew very weak, I believe others were divinely placed in my life to give me strength.

"You have been given a difficult cross to bear, but this is the challenge God gave you," Aunt Tina said. "A unique challenge designed just for you. Not to take away your light, but to allow your light to shine brighter than you could imagine. You may not see it this way, but this isn't punishment. It's a responsibility. Continue to be strong, Daniel. Use your story and what you continue to overcome. You have only seen the beginning."

Even a stranger once told me that "God will give you a test to give you a testimony."

I thought about how many times I had heard that I would overcome all I had been dealt. I thought about how at one point I believed I would, also. I didn't know how I was going to do this, but I wanted to believe that they were speaking things into existence that I couldn't see any longer. I looked at her and replied, "You're right."

We prayed and loved on each other before the hospital staff called me back. Unlike my previous surgeries, there was minimal prep before the biopsy. I put on the hospital robe and waited in the room. The anesthesiologists arrived and explained the process of extracting the bone marrow from my pelvis.

"We will numb the insertion area and drill a needle into your hip, where bone marrow will be extracted for testing," he explained.

"Are we ready to get started?" The doctor reached out to shake my hand. I grabbed his hand and replied, "Yeah, let's do it."

I was rolled on a gurney down the hallway. We arrived at the procedure room early and had to wait in the hallway until the room was prepared. As I lay there on the hospital bed, another young African American male walked into the hallway. He sat about ten feet away from where I waited. He appeared to be concerned as he went through his phone searching for information.

"I'm about to make a call so let me know if I'm disturbing you," he said to me while lifting the phone to his ear. I let him know that there was no problem. As he sat on the phone, I could tell he was observing me. I tried to ignore the fact that he continued to look in my direction, even while in mid-conversation. I hoped that I would be pulled into the room before his conversation ended, but little to my surprise, he hung up the phone almost as soon as I had that thought. I avoided eye contact, which wasn't hard for me. As I stared at the ceiling, I heard a voice address me.

"Hey, brother. If you don't mind, I would like to pray for you. Please let me know if I'm being intrusive, but God keeps telling me to say something to you and I don't want to be disobedient."

Surprised by his words, I agreed and reached out for his hand. He asked me my name and what I was in the hospital dealing with. I tried to be as concise as possible and explain why I was there. I started off by telling him about my vision issues back in 2014 and what transpired up to this point. I was close enough to see the look on his face. It was the look of concern, amazement, and utter disbelief.

"Dude, and I been sitting here trying to find a reason not to talk to you. Really, I just didn't want to disturb your quiet time. Brother, you have really touched me. I'm so sorry to hear about everything that you are going through."

As he stood beside me in the hallway, we talked for about 10 minutes. He told me that he was there supporting a friend who had several health issues. We both talked about hardships and how God can use them to put you in position to help yourself and others.

"Look, I know they will be out here to get you soon so let me pray for you before we get interrupted," he said as we held hands. He said a powerful prayer over my life and over my health. He prayed for my family, friends, and for me to use my circumstances to bless others. I got slightly emotional as he spoke blessings into my life. Not long after he finished the prayer, the tech came out of the procedure room.

"We finished right in time," I said. Before we parted, he wished me the best, and I did the same for him. As they began to roll me into the room, he turned around and called back out to me.

"I'm going to be praying for you. Tell me your name, again."

"Daniel Drumwright," I said.

His tone vaguely changed, indicating that he was slightly perplexed when he asked, "Are you any relation to Pastor Drumwright?" I smiled and replied, "He's my brother." Because my brother was very well-known and liked in the community, I knew the encounter made a more significant impression for him.

"Your brother is awesome, and you… You are an inspiration. Keep going."

I nodded my head and wished him well. As the staff rolled me away, I watched the broken image of the man I had just spoken to walk in the opposite direction. To think, I didn't even want to communicate with this man. I didn't even remember him giving me his name.

The procedure concluded, and I was discharged shortly after entering recovery. I would like to say that the good energy I got at the hospital stayed with me thereafter, but that wasn't the case. I tried to focus on making some objectives for myself in the days afterwards. They all sounded good, but my heart wasn't there. I tried to be hopeful and positive toward my outlook, but instead I reverted back to my antagonistic, depressed, and unhappy self. I tried to focus on my beautiful bride-to-be and becoming a family, but that didn't keep my mind from wondering if our relationship would get better or worse, especially when I was alone. Or maybe I didn't try hard enough. I just couldn't get out of the rut that I was in.

Chapter 41
Broken Mirrors

I continued to battle with mental health. My mind never rested, I found it more and more difficult to sleep at night, and contemplating ways to end it all routinely popped in my thoughts.

I remember thinking about mortality as I walked the dog in our neighborhood one evening. Our street ran parallel to the main road, which was two lanes and always busy. I walked toward the main road and stood there as cars passed by. I thought about what it would be like if I just stepped out into traffic. But I didn't. I reminded myself of the promise I made to Brandy. We made a decision to be life partners, and I didn't want to cheat her or myself. Unfortunately, even though that promise was becoming less of a priority for me as my mental health and self-worth plummeted, I still stopped myself from walking into traffic that day.

On another occasion that fall, I pulled out my .380 automatic pistol that was tucked away in the back of our closet to hide from Blake. I only had three rounds left, as it had been nearly a year since the last time I went to the gun range. I loaded the three rounds in the clip and laid the gun on top of the fire pit under the gazebo. After a few moments, I cocked the gun and put it to my head, making sound effects that emulated a gun going off and reminding myself that Uber is just a request away.

Unlike earlier in the year with the neck tie, I had thought out steps I would take if I were to take my life. I wouldn't want to do anything like that for Brandy or Blake to find me. I would take an Uber to a remote location.

I had a plan if it all became unbearable. All of my pain would be gone, but I knew that it wouldn't fix anything. The pain would just be beginning for my family and friends. As selfish as it was, I found myself less bothered by this thought.

It had only been a few weeks since my biopsy, and I had gone from encouraged, to doubtful, to despondent, to disconnected. Meanwhile, Brandy remained her normal festive self and decorated the home with fall attire, which included bales of hay and a scarecrow. My favorite time of the year drifted by as I struggled to deal with my health concerns and mounting depression.

"What are we eating for dinner," Brandy asked as I stood in front of the TV taking in the college football game. I acted oblivious to her, as I didn't care what we had. I walked away slowly, as I was still sore from the biopsy. I walked to the bathroom and shut the door behind me. I didn't have to use the bathroom. I just didn't want to deal with anything. I sat on the toilet and continued my thoughts. While sitting there I nodded off, dreaming about all of the fall events I loved. Instead of enjoying myself, I stood in the mist of everything happening with a stoic expression, as I looked through a window back at the image of my previous self. That most confident and accomplished version of myself stared back in disappointment.

There was a knock at the door. I was startled as the knocking awoke me. I stood up and headed to the sink, as if I had actually used the restroom.

"Are you okay with pizza? It should be on its way," Blake said from the other side of the door.

"That works," I replied while washing my hands. We ate on the couch and talked about birthday plans, hosting an Ugly Christmas Sweater Party, and the Thanksgiving holiday.

"We don't have to do a lot for my birthday. We can celebrate my birthday at the Ugly Christmas Sweater Party," I suggested as I took a bite of my pizza. We discussed food options, decorations, and group games we all could play. We joked about the type of sweaters we would get made and finalized plans.

We then began discussing plans for Thanksgiving Day, figuring out how we were going to split time at multiple places. I had two sides of the family that had Thanksgiving, but there was no way I could expect Brandy to go to both meals and still make it to her family's dinner. With a bit of disappointment, we decided to split holidays with our families. Brandy could tell I was disappointed and asked, "Are you upset?" I shook my head no, but I proceeded to have attitude. She got irritated.

"I think you are being really inconsiderate. Do you really expect us to go everywhere on the holiday? Don't you think we want to spend time with my family? I don't want to spend the holiday ripping and running!"

Her words infuriated me. I clinched the blanket we sat on as she continued. She looked at me and paused. The look on my face must have caught her attention.

"What? Am I not supposed to say anything and you expect…"

Before she could finish, I erupted. I didn't expect anything other than what we had discussed, even though I wasn't enthused. I knew her words weren't meant to be crass, but her declaration that I was being inconsiderate was the flame that lit the wick. Blake and Minx watched in confusion as I raised my voice.

"You go do what you want! I don't need you to take me anywhere! I didn't ask you for shit and don't expect shit! I'll stay my ass home! I don't want to be in front of anyone like this anyway!"

My heart raced as we spoke harshly toward one another. She accused me of being selfish and trying to guilt her for me having to ration my family time. I came back at her.

"No, you assume that because I have emotions about it. Sorry if I'm disappointed. If I don't prefer your suggestions, then I am going against you. You need to figure out how to deal with opposition, because…"

Brandy interrupted, "Because what?!"

I looked at her for a moment and replied, "How are you going to tell me how I should feel? I have had my whole life turned upside-down! And I try not to complain to anyone! Do you even realize that?"

Brandy looked in silence as I continued my rant.

"Do you think I want my woman to be burdened by me?! I don't ask you for shit, because I don't want you to take care of me! That's my job! I'm supposed to take care of you all!"

I stood and left the living room to be alone. I had only taken a small bite of my pizza, but I no longer had an appetite. Brandy asked me to stay, but I didn't know what else to say. My blow up had nothing to do with our plans, but somehow the conversation led to an argument. No matter how I was feeling, things rarely seemed to come out right. I felt misunderstood and worthless, as I stood in the garage with tears silently falling from my eyes. I wasn't used to taking things personal so often, but everything seemed to bother me more and more. I had grown more sensitive as time went on, even when there wasn't much to be sensitive about. While I was disappointed with the way I had responded, I was more disappointed with why I responded that way.

After a short while, the door leading into the garage cracked opened, startling me as I stood there.

"I'm heading upstairs. I was just letting you know," Brandy said while peeking through the opening.

"Okay, I will be up," I replied.

There was a lot that Brandy could have said in response to me, but she didn't. Some of the things I said were merited and others not so much. I was so bothered by everything else going on that I let this situation get out of hand. Then, instead of talking it out, I walked out on her. I had tried to be normal, do normal things, and make normal plans. Still, nothing was what I would call "normal." I didn't believe I could feel any worse, but I did. My spirit fell to an all-time low. I felt like I should have been better off, though. I wanted to be better off. I knew I had to do something different, even though I didn't know what that was.

Thanksgiving came and we spent time with my mother's side of the family, then left to be with Brandy's family. Everyone showered me with love, as they always did. And while I appreciated and valued everyone's support, I still felt out of place and not quite myself. All my life I wanted to make everyone proud of me. Now, all I wanted was to be the confident, witty, personable, and full of life Daniel I was before. Instead, I found myself reserved, uneasy, and melancholy. I wanted to engage our family, but I couldn't get out of my own head and just connect. It was almost as if I was in a bubble, watching my family celebrate the holidays with each other.

Chapter 42
Hanging with my Dunnies

My birthday came, which we celebrated along with our Ugly Christmas Sweater Party. It was a hit. Several of our friends came and enjoyed music, food, games, drinks, and other extracurriculars. We even had the fire pit going and made S'mores.

"How you been feeling Dunny? You lookin' good," Nick said as Tracy and I followed him and Decosta to the patio.

"I'm okay. Still adjusting, but you know," I replied. I knew I could talk to my friends about anything. Never did I have to wonder if I would be judged. Decosta passed the Black & Mild cigar, and I took a drag. I followed the cloud of smoke through the air as best I could. The cool crisp air was perfect. The moment felt familiar, like the nights we had going out in the past.

"Real talk, this has been the hardest thing I've ever done. It has been really difficult to be hopeful, but I have so many people on my side. It's hard to listen to the cheers and be positive when you're hurting, but I just keep going. I can't let y'all down. I just know this can't be it. From losing my sight to having leukemia, I'm still here. I know there's more to life."

They all reassured me that my thoughts and feelings were merited.

"I know you've been down. You had life pulled right from under you, but I'm proud of you. You could find any reason to give up, but you haven't. I talk about you to the boys often. I know you don't see your situation as favorable, but it's definitely inspiring. Anyone can be motivated by how far you've come," Tracy encouraged me. I nodded in agreement as I passed the Black & Mild.

"Yeah, I can be a persistent and stubborn ass, if I must say. I guess I don't know how to give up. I admit I have to do better about how I've been dealing. I will. I promise y'all that."

Nick replied, "Don't do it for us. We got you. Do it for you."

We finished the cigar and headed back inside to rejoin the fun. Nick and I headed to the kitchen to grab a bite, while Decosta and Tracy made their way to the garage. That weekend was what I needed to get the ground back under my feet. It was nothing big, just a fun weekend with plenty going on to occupy my time and mind. Of course, my health and sight were the topic of much conversation, and I actually felt comfortable addressing it.

"Man, no way?! I would have died three times," one of Brandy's longtime friends suggested as she listened in. A small group developed as I continued telling my story. I had shared the detailed story about my circumstances with only a few people before that night. I was humbled to see other's reactions and responses to what I had shared. I hadn't thought about how few people really knew the full story.

"But it's your attitude, man. You would never have known that you've gone through so much the way you carry yourself. Bro, I am inspired," my close friend Bryan Torrain said. I thought about his words and had to be honest.

"While I have put on a smile and remained positive around you all, I must admit that I have at times almost given up on myself. I might have given up if it hadn't been for family and friends; you all. God sent me people, good people to keep me going. It's not what happens to you, it's how you respond. I'm just trying to remember that."

For the second time in a month, I had the opportunity to tell others about finding purpose. In particular were those conversations I had with my former youth pastor, Damien. He was one of my biggest supporters long before leukemia and loss of sight. From music and video, to my career opportunities, he always expressed how excited he was for the opportunities that would come my way.

"Tap into them tools God gave you and tell your story. They're going to see God all in that bad boy! Know that!"

***

My aunt took me to an appointment at Cornea Consultants where I learned that I needed cataract surgery. A cataract is a clouding of the lens of the eye, and healthy lenses are typically clear. My cataracts prevented the doctors from seeing clearly to the back of my eye. While procedures had not been performed on every part of my eye, I believe every part of my eye had been impacted by my surgeries. Early on in the process, one of my doctors explained that I would likely need to get my lenses replaced because of all the work being done on my eyes made them vulnerable.

Cataract surgery was being recommended for me to maximize any potential vision and to help monitor my progress. At this point, I was just going through the motions, and I didn't think it would actually improve my situation. But I went along with it anyway.

We set the cataract surgery for December 30 and made our way home shortly afterward. On the way home, my aunt and I discussed my recent attitude and pessimism.

"If you don't want to do any more surgeries after this, I understand. I know it has been hard on your spirit, but don't let this change who you are," she said. "You got a lot to be grateful for. You have this beautiful woman who wants to see you through all of this. We want to see you through all of this, but you have to want it. I just pray that you hold on to your faith."

I was starting to have these conversations far too often, both with myself and others. I knew that people would start taking notice to my attitude change. I could play the role for a little longer, but I couldn't fake it forever.

"I know I have a lot to be grateful for. I'm still here and I know that's for a reason, but I am struggling to find purpose, and I'm far from being at peace. It's a struggle identifying as disabled. I don't want to be different, but I am and that bothers me," I said as we traveled down Interstate 24.

"Baby, you are as whole as you have always been, but you have to own this! Accept where you are! Once you do that, you will find what you're looking for. You might not think you are who you once were, but you are the same person you have always been. Disability or no disability, but you have to know that."

I gave Aunt Maychelle a kiss goodbye as we got to my home. I went into the weekend with a lot to think about. It was just a few weeks away from Christmas and my one-year anniversary of losing my sight. I had imagined this triumphant comeback story from all the adversity I had been dealt. How different things actually were! While there was no immediate fix for the conditions and circumstances I faced, I kept coming back to the conversations I had with my therapist about finding a way to accept and make peace with all that I had been through. I hoped to be cleared for physical activity soon, so that I would have another outlet to channel my energy and relieve pressure. Ultimately, I had to learn how to restore my faith – in myself, in God, in my ability to be the head of a household, and be successful in all these roles after having to adapt and adjust the vision I had for my life. I still had many milestones to achieve in the meantime.

***

The weekend went by fast. We had no big plans, since we did it big the weekend before. We sat in our bedroom Sunday night and had dinner. We discussed plans for the Christmas holiday, which included going to Opryland Hotel to see the Christmas lights. I was quite sleepy and lethargic. I figured the leukemia medication was weighing on me.

"Yeah baby, I'm going to go ahead and lay it down," I said to Brandy as I got under the covers.

"Okay, baby," she replied.

I easily drifted off to sleep. Usually, when I was asleep, I slept lightly. But this night, I felt like a rock in water. I started to dream that I could hear the dog barking and pulling at my shirt. My clothing felt damp, as if I had been running through the rain. I heard Brandy's voice, but I could not make out anything she was saying. There was no image of what was going on, just a moon in the sky with clouds moving in front of it. The clouds continued to accumulate until the moon was completely hidden and everything was black.

I slowly began to wake up from my dream, I started to come to, and I could see three figures in front of me. I heard an unfamiliar beeping noise, and I knew that it wasn't my insulin pump.

"Alright buddy. Can you tell me your name now?" an older gentleman's voice said to me. I felt poking in my right hand.

"Blood sugar is 54," a lady who sounded nothing like Brandy said. My blood sugar had gone low while I was sleeping, and Brandy called for an ambulance. It was the first time she'd ever seen me unresponsive due to having low blood sugar. I didn't have my glasses near me, but I could faintly see Brandy speaking with an emergency medical technician and wiping her eyes.

"Blood sugar is 71. It's coming up."

What seemed like a few minutes to me had actually been an hour and a half ordeal. After I declined the EMTs' offer to be taken to the hospital, they gave Brandy some information pertaining to my blood sugars and suggestions to keep it up during the night. I could tell that she was quite shaken up. They eventually removed the needle from my hand that was administering glucose to my bloodstream.

"I know you don't want to go to the hospital, but make sure you keep something close in case your sugar goes low again. Are you sure you're okay?" the EMT asked.

I nodded and thanked the three of them for helping me. Not long after, they left. Brandy reentered our bedroom and stood facing the wall. She began crying aloud. She was frightened and inconsolable. Though I had been through so much, nothing could prepare me or Brandy for everything that kept coming up. At that moment, things got real.

Chapter 43
Hand-Eye

Brandy paced back and forth across the bedroom.

"Come on, Daniel."

With tears coming down her face, she tried to gather herself. She was shook. I spoke calmly to her, attempting to comfort her.

"Brandy, I am okay. It's not the first time this has happened, but it's the first time in a long time," I tried to explain, but Brandy's mood didn't allow for it. She struggled to get her words together. As embarrassed as I was, I only wanted her to listen and hear me out. She eventually let me speak.

"Brandy, I'm sorry. This is what happens when my sugar goes extremely low. It doesn't do this often, but it happens," I said to her.

"How do we prevent this from happening? You have the insulin pump and sensor," she replied.

I explained that even though I had this equipment, it wouldn't prevent low blood sugar.

"The hope is to catch it before it gets too low. I did not have my sensor on and I was asleep, so catching it before it got too low would be nearly impossible. Baby, there is no fix to this. At times, my blood sugar will go low. Just because you wear your seat belt doesn't mean you won't get hurt in an accident. The same goes for this," I said the most convincing way I could. She was not satisfied with my answers, which left me frustrated. As she continued to reply, she sensed my frustration.

"Daniel, I understand you will have lows, but you don't know how this affects me. You don't know how this affects us. I knew that I was taking on a lot when you were first diagnosed and this all happened, but you have to do better."

Her suggestion that I had not done enough angered me. She continued.

"What good is your sensor if it's not on? I'm just saying, look at it from my perspective."

I interrupted her saying, "What does that have to do with my blood sugar going low? It happens. You obviously don't know how diabetes works. You're the health professional, right?"

I was sure that questioning her knowledge rubbed her the wrong way, but I was determined to make my point.

"Daniel, you have to deal with this! And it's a lot to deal with! You have to admit that you can do more to make sure these issues don't keep coming up. Things happen, and I get that. No one could have predicted that this would happen to you. Life has been unfair to you, but what other choice do you have at this point but to do everything you can? You have to do anything and everything possible, Daniel. I'm here for you, but I can't do this for you. And I can't promise you I will stay if how you've been dealing with this doesn't improve. I won't."

I wanted to respond to her, but I didn't have the energy. I knew that things with Brandy and I would eventually get to this point, but it definitely wasn't what I wanted. I was so disappointed with everything that I mentally checked out. About that time, Blake walked into the room. We had been dealing with so much that I forgot Blake was home.

"What's going on? I was asleep and then I heard some people talking. Now, you and Daniel are mad," Blake said. We explained that it was nothing and asked him to go back to bed. As I watched him walk out of the room, I began to feel guilty.

"Brandy, I'm sorry. I know this scared you, but this is not a normal occurrence. With all the changes, my body is trying to adjust. It's a lot, but I got it," I said before Brandy interrupted me.

"You think you have it all figured out, but you don't. You have been different for a while and I'm not talking about your health. I mean you. I understand you have been through hell, but you need to look inside yourself and ask, 'Am I doing everything I can? Am I trying to do all I can?' You need to be honest with yourself. You have to get this right."

Brandy walked into our bathroom and closed the door behind her. I listened as she quietly cried from the other side of the door. I knew she needed time to herself, so I made my way into the hallway and braced myself against the banister. As I stood there trying to process what had just happened, I felt a furry nudge against my leg. It was Minx, making her way up my calf. I picked her up and sat at the top of the steps.

"Yeah Minx, I ain't shit. I have been able to keep this lie going, but not anymore."

I was living a lie. I was trying to convince everyone that I was managing my life well, working through my problems, adjusting, being prayerful, overcoming barriers and redefining myself as a disabled young man. It's a lie I was telling myself and everyone else.

I thought I had the outside world fooled, because I only dealt with them in doses. But Brandy was coming home to me every day. She saw through my charade. She knew I wasn't doing as well as I pretended to be.

I thought I could turn a lie into the truth. I thought I could convince myself to believe in the idea of "hope" that I was telling others about. And somehow, I would believe the words I was proclaiming, and propel myself back to a place of faith.

I talked to Minx as if she had advice to give me. Her big eyes peered at me, like she was sympathetic to my feelings. I carried her downstairs where we finished our conversation.

"She's right. I have been indifferent. Maybe I should stop before I take them through anything else. Maybe I'm being selfish by allowing them to endure all of this. Who goes through this? Who openly welcomes this as a part of their life? Brandy probably doesn't want me to feel like she's giving up on me. Some wouldn't have thought twice. They would have been gone long ago," I said as I sat in the living room.

Without warning, Minx jumped from my lap and scurried up the stairs. As I sat alone, my mind went back to times where I thought about taking my own life. I rationalized it, thinking how everyone would have one less burden.

Why am I in this hell? God, just end it. I can't keep doing this. I don't want this, I thought as I sat sulking.

I had gone into that dark place, once again. I never thought life would get this hard for me, but maybe I should have tried harder. Given more of myself. Maybe I should have continued to see my therapist or been more engaged with Brandy and the wedding planning, or even found a support group to help deal with my anger and frustration.

Though I hadn't given all I could, I just didn't have interest in the future and what it may bring any longer.

As I continued in my downward spiral, my phone began to ring. It was my brother, David.

"Hey, Daniel! It's David. I got a call from Brandy while I was at work. Is everything okay?" He had been working a later shift during the holiday season. Hearing his voice brought me to tears.

"No, Dave. Things aren't okay. Can you come, please? I mean, I know it's late, but..." I said before being interrupted.

"I'm on my way. I should be there in less than 30 minutes."

I listened for David to pull up to the house. When I heard his car door close, I waited for him to walk to the door. I opened the storm door and tears flooded my face. He grabbed me and held on to me as I cried.

"It's okay, Daniel. Just talk to me. What happened?"

I explained to him what happened. David was quite familiar with my diabetic episodes. The first one I had where I was unresponsive was the summer after our mother passed. We were home in the middle of the night, and David found me leaning against the wall talking to myself. He immediately called the ambulance and Aunt Maychelle, who lived close at that time. Because my father worked out of the state, David knew he had a responsibility to me, just as I had to him.

"Daniel, you know I know what it is. We've been through this a few times in the past. Give you some juice and you're back up and popping," David said trying to cheer me up. This time things were different, though.

"David, I don't know. I'm so tired of this. I'm so tired of feeling worthless. I just want this to be over. I want to be me. I don't want to do this anymore," I said while trying not to yell. David wrapped his arm around my shoulder and pulled me close and spoke calmly to me.

"Daniel, do you remember when mom died? Do you remember what you said to me," he asked.

"You told me that Momma wants us to keep pushing, no matter what. And you told me you would have my back every step of the way. And you have."

Tears soaked his shirt as I lay my head on his shoulder. As I raised my head from his shoulder, he looked at me and said, "Daniel, I got you. We got you. Just don't give up. I don't know what I'd do without you."

Tears streamed down his face. As I looked at him, I didn't see the 28-year-old man the he had become. I saw the 15-year-old kid I comforted that morning our mom died. We sat and talked for about an hour, and as we revisited memories of our life.

I began to be honest with myself. I was dwelling in self-pity. I wasn't trying to adjust. I wasn't happy that my conditions were stable. I wasn't trying to overcome. I wanted things to get better on my time. I said a lot of things that sounded good, but I wasn't being real with myself. I wanted things to go back to the way they were. I hoped my faith and outlook would add some good karma to my situation. Instead of a swift recovery, treatment would likely be a part of my new normal for some time, and there were no guarantees that things would get any better. I wasn't just legally blind. I was low vision. My sight was that poor, and there was nothing I could do about it, but stay the course. No matter how good of a person I thought I was, how many salads I ate, or hours I spent in the gym, I was not in control of the process. All I could do is step up to the plate and swing the bat at the curveballs I had been thrown.

I awoke around 4:00 a.m. on the couch next to David, like we had done so many times in our childhood. Still embarrassed about the incident, I contemplated going upstairs to lie in the bed with Brandy. I didn't know if she was still bothered by the episode and whether I should let her be. I sat and thought about whether she would even want me close to her. Then I looked at David as he slept and began to remember the thought I had just a few hours before. I knew I had to address these issues and not hide behind my pride. I turned the living room light off and headed upstairs. I got to the room and stood near her side of the bed. I watched her as she slept, wondering whether I should get in the bed, as I didn't want to awaken her. I got as close to her as I could and got on one knee. I carefully placed my hand on her hip, closed my eyes, and began to quietly pray.

Dear God, I have been selfish and I have not been the man that everyone has known me to be. I have failed to be the man that I have told myself and everyone else I would be. And I am sorry. I have not lived by the sayings I recite time and time again. I have allowed this to change who I am on the inside, and I am ashamed. You have given me family, friends, and a beautiful woman who have all stayed by my side. They have held me up, and I have many times kept myself down. I have been so angry with You, God, for allowing me to go through this, but I should be mad at myself. I am here in part because I let myself get here.

Brandy began to move. I thought about moving my hand off of her, but I left it on her hip. I knew I was lucky to have someone who loved me so much, no matter how unhappy I was with myself.

God, please bless this woman. She is awesome. I know You put her in my life. She holds me accountable. She expects a lot from me and helps me push myself. She gets on my nerves, but I love her for doing so. You definitely knew what You were doing. You have shown Yourself through her and everyone else You've put in my life.

I stood from her side and walked around to my side of the bed. I got under the covers, lying there with my thoughts. I continued praying.

Thank You for another chance. Thank You for putting people in my life to help me and remind me of the grace that has been granted to me. Thank You for the reminder. I will do better. Amen.

As I closed my eyes, Brandy placed her hand on mine. I came in closer, wrapping my arm and leg around her. We lay there for several minutes until her alarm went off. She grabbed her phone to turn the alarm silent. I moved over to allow her room to get up, but she grabbed me and pulled me back close. I wrapped my arms tightly around her and we lay there for another hour. We finally got up and talked.

"I'm sorry for my recent behavior," I began. "I know we're supposed to be planning a wedding, but I feel like I have left that on you. You were going to plan most of this anyway, but I have spent more time focusing on all the negativity going on in my life. I should be more excited and involved. I have been selfish. I have been down. But I'm here, now. We have so much more to look forward to, so I will try to enjoy this time with you. Because we will never get it back. I want you to be happy you made the decision to marry me. I truly want to be the partner you deserve and I yearn to be."

We discussed the incident from the night before and what we could do to make sure these issues were few and far between. She had to go to work, so we decided to finish the conversation later. David awoke from his sleep and checked on us before leaving.

I watched them both pull off and I closed the garage once her car was out of sight. I entered the kitchen to make a cup of coffee and retreated to the bonus room. I was relieved Brandy and I seemed to be okay, but I had some things that I needed to deal with internally if I was ever going to feel secure again. I researched some strategies to help deal with internal conflicts. I found an article with some helpful tools and questions to ask oneself.

"How am I feeling and what led me to feel this way?"

I typed up my feelings in a text to myself.

"Frustrated. Lost. Hampered. Unreliable. Boxed-in. Suffocated. Alone. Angry. Disappointed. Forgotten. Failure. Betrayed."

I stopped to read my list. I had several other feelings in mind, but these summed it up. I began to think about the second part of the question. It seemed like a simple question, but I kept coming back to my ailments. As much as my health issues had impacted my life, they weren't the reason I had been stuck in a rut. I spent the next few days focusing on finding peace and remedying myself. I had considered going back to the therapist, but I didn't want to until I did some real soul searching. I didn't want to go through the motions. I talked to my older brother and father that week about dealing with grief. My father and I spoke of his late mother and how knowing she was no longer in pain gave him peace.

If my sight failed to improve, could I ever get over the anger and frustration? I wanted to be a good husband, father, and person, but could I fake happiness? The problem was that I knew there would come a time when I could no longer fool myself or others by faking happiness.

***

I turned on sports news, as I often did, and they were revisiting stories that had been previously covered. One in particular caught my attention.

"I remember this one," I said to myself as I watched. It was the story of a 12-year-old USC fan who lost both of his eyes to cancer. He was now a student at the University of Southern California and on the football team as a long snapper. I watched as he spoke about getting through the initial shock of being totally blind. He also addressed the challenges he faced relearning certain tasks and the rough days that followed. Nevertheless, he adjusted. More importantly, he refused to feel sorry for himself and accepted his journey. I sat there in thought about what I had just watched.

Wow. This kid plays golf, is in college, has a social life, and even plays football. This kid is living the best life he can, despite no control over his circumstances. I, on the other hand, have let all this stifle my happiness and growth. I haven't done much of anything to get past any of this. I haven't followed through on the things I started. I give up before I give myself a chance. I can't change my reality. So instead of accepting it, I've cursed it. I haven't taken responsibility for my shortfalls. I am responsible, just as much as leukemia.

I paused as I continued with my thoughts.

I haven't accepted being low vision. I haven't owned my new normal. Acceptance. That's the only way I'm going to start moving forward.

I went to the bathroom and looked through my battered eyes at my reflection. I was so disappointed in myself. I could no longer play victim.

Wow, Daniel. You've been mad at God. You've been mad at the Devil. You've been mad at leukemia and diabetes. You've been mad at the world. You should be mad at yourself. You didn't listen to your body. You didn't keep your appointments. Honestly, you treated your appointments as if they were an inconvenience; even unnecessary. You thought you had it all under control. These ailments have done a number on your health, but you choose how to deal with it. Who knows? Maybe all this would have happened anyway, but you can't go back now. Life ain't fair, but you only get one. Make the best of it. Accept it and keep going.

A few nights later, after I had time to think, I was ready to talk to Brandy and come clean.

"I'm sorry for how I've been, but I'm ready to take responsibility. I am ready to accept my new reality and learn to adapt and move forward. I made that promise to you and everyone else that I haven't kept up to this point. I won't break my promise."

Brandy usually had a lot to say, but not so much this time. She smiled and rubbed my back. She looked me in the face and gave me a kiss.

"Daniel, I just want us to have a long life together. I know there will be some things that happen, but everything you have can be managed. Just promise you will do that. Not for me, though. For yourself." She apologized for the way she responded the night of my diabetic episode, but reiterated the need for me to be on top of all my health issues.

I grabbed her hand and replied, "I'm doing this for all of us. I'm doing it for my friends, my family, the dog, but I'm doing it for myself, too."

I knew it would take more than just doing it for myself. Accepting that I would likely be low vision for the rest of my life would be difficult, so I needed more purpose. I wasn't sure what that purpose was exactly, but they were my motivation. I wanted to make them proud. I wanted to enrich their lives. I couldn't do that feeling sorry for myself. I didn't want to be limited by my disability, so that meant not letting it. The truth was that I already had all the motivation and support I needed. I just couldn't see past myself.

Chapter 44
Baby Steps

On Tuesday, November 17, Dr. Schneider cleared me to return to the gym to do cardio and lift moderate weights. I called Brandy after the appointment and told her she would have to take me to the gym near our home to get a membership. I also suggested that we start going to the gym together like we did when we first started dating. She had already planned to enroll, so we went Saturday morning.

We attended church the following morning, went for brunch afterward, and went to the gym that night. I hadn't worked out in almost a year and it showed. I did more cardio than anything and got in a really good workout. I needed to get in shape before our wedding, but my biggest concern would be how to get to and from the gym on my own. I didn't want to have to wait for Brandy, but I hadn't thought too far ahead.

"Maybe you can drop me off in the morning sometimes. I will hang out until my dad can come and take me home," I said to Brandy as we exited the gym. She agreed while trying to think of other options.

"Do you think you could walk home?"

I hadn't considered it, but the gym was only a 10-minute walk from the house. The road I would have to walk was two lanes with no sidewalk, though. Before I could answer, she said, "Don't push yourself too fast. We'll figure it out."

***

It was time for the holidays again, and we were taking full advantage of the opportunity to relax and enjoy the season. Brandy was off work for three days for Christmas break. We ordered pizza and prepared cookies to eat while watching Christmas movies.

Brandy entered the bedroom to change from her work scrubs. I walked up from behind her and wrapped my arms around her waist. She grabbed my arms and pulled herself closer. I began kissing her neck and ear.

"You gonna make me burn the cookies," she said as she reached back to wrap her arm around my neck. She turned to look at me and gave me a kiss on the lips. I pushed my hip into hers and replied, "I'm not concerned about those cookies." She laughed as she pulled away.

We visited with family on Christmas Day. I was showered with love as everyone was happy to see me in good spirits. Though I was still adjusting, I was more at peace about where I was and my hopes continued to grow.

The morning after Christmas, I cleaned up all the gift-wrapping paper and boxes from the previous day. It was unusually warm for a December morning with the weather feeling really pleasant as I took the bag of trash out. Brandy and I made plans to go to the gym that afternoon.

"I can drop you off, but I won't be back from running errands and visiting with family for at least a few hours," she said. "I can pick you up on my way back around 4 p.m. Or do you feel okay using a ride share service?"

I told her I could take a ride share home if all else failed. The gym was only 0.7 miles from our house, and she had to pass it on the way home. But I didn't want to inconvenience her or wait longer than necessary to get picked up.

For the first time since I was 12-years-old, I was intimidated to walk into the gym alone. I gave myself a pep talk and was determined to take my time getting reacclimated to the environment. I thoroughly stretched and started blaring my music playlist through my headphones. I used the stair-climbing exercise machine for 30 minutes and did a light-weight circuit. To cool down, I walked on the treadmill for another 15 minutes and headed to the hydro-massage bed.

I had been at the gym for an hour and a half, so I pulled out my phone and reading glasses to call a ride. I entered my home location and hit "submit."

"$6.15? That's not a lot, but I don't even stay a mile from here. My membership is only $10 a month."

I started to get annoyed, feeling limited by my disability once again. I didn't want to spend a bunch of money getting around, but it didn't seem like I had a choice.

Unless I just walk home, I thought.

I thought about how unsafe it would be walking up a busy road with no sidewalk. I had seen plenty of people do it in the past, but I was sure none of them were nearly blind. I was happy just to be out of the house and wasn't about to let this bother me. I had made a huge step.

Oh well, I will just have to...

Before I finished my thought about calling a ride to pick me up, "Don't Play," a song by Travis Scott, came on. As it played through my headphones, the high energy from the song fed into me. Maybe it wasn't the safest decision to make, but I needed to challenge myself. For the last 12 months, the biggest thing holding me back had been myself.

"You got this," I said aloud.

I gathered my things, put on my hoodie, and stepped outside the gym into the comfortably warm weather. I walked down the hill to Una-Antioch Pike and took a hard look at the cars traveling the road. I took a deep breath.

"You got this!"

I walked onto the narrow shoulder of the road. I stumbled a few times, as the shoulder was uneven, but I took my time. I could see the cars coming toward my direction as they got closer and was able to keep a safe distance. I panned up and down to be sure I remained on the shoulder and out of the street where cars were steadily passing by.

This walk was symbolic for me. Even with the best support system in the world, the past year was a journey that I ultimately had to take alone, within myself, to find my true sense of purpose and manhood, and recalibrate my center around my faith and my family. As much as I wanted to move forward, do better, and feel like a confident and redefined person, I was still quite afraid of what was ahead of me.

Fear was a significant presence in my spirit. Fear of the unknown. Fear of failure and not being able to overcome. Would I be able to adjust? Would people be patient with my short comings? Would I have to fight society's inability to be more understanding, more accommodating, more accepting, and more inclusive?

The alternative seemed much easier: Do nothing and shy away into the shadows of society.

When I was a child, I was in school with students who had disabilities. I was nice to them, but not overly compassionate. I was not astute enough to understand that, while they were different in some ways, we were all the same in the ways that really matter. We all wanted to feel included.

I never fathomed that I would end up being someone who needed extra help or consideration in a society that is really impatient and unfriendly to people with disabilities. There are myriad hurdles to jump that people without physical ailments don't have to think twice about.

I didn't want to accept that my situation was real. It took a long time for me to reject the notion that it was all a bad dream from which I was certain to spontaneously awake. But there was a point when I knew the only thing I had absolute control over was to learn to accept the challenge and go full steam ahead. Even if my "full steam ahead" was simply putting one foot in front of the other. However it looked, moving forward was the only option. As I began to make intentional steps, not only did I reach small milestones and see that my goals were attainable, I also realized that many of the things I feared did not even exist.

Ten minutes later, I found myself at the entrance of my subdivision. My street was the first one off Una-Antioch Pike, so I hit my block and made it down the home stretch. I entered my driveway a short walk later and opened the garage. I dropped my bag off in the house and let Minx out to enjoy the nice weather. I looked as best I could in the direction of Una-Antioch Pike from my front yard and I smiled.

What the hell was I so scared of?

Why did I second guess myself?

Why did I let pride stand in the way for so long and hinder me from asking for help?

Why was I afraid that I couldn't adjust to society. Society is going to have to adjust to me!

Going forward, I will be strong and courageous and take the opportunity not to just tell my story but to be an advocate for societal change.

I never thought I'd go blind and be forced to revise the way my life worked. But, I learned that challenges are just opportunities to overcome. When I examined my life – my finances, education, relationships, health, faith, and self-esteem – it required me to belief in, trust, and champion myself. I never would have known what I could overcome, until I was challenged beyond what I could have imagined.

Pushing through my extreme visual deficit and being able to thrive despite my disability empowered me. It gave me a perspective that hopefully enables me to inspire and positively impact others. My ups and downs were no doubt volatile, but I chose not to give up. I identified processes that would allow me to function more efficiently, and I made the best out of my situation.

While I was celebrating my successful walk home, my phone rang. It was Brandy.

"Hey, baby," I answered.

"Hey, I'm headed to the house. Do you need me to stop and pick you up from the gym?" she asked.

I grinned and replied, "No, I made it home." I could tell she was happy that I took the initiative to get home.

"Ok good. So, you called a ride share?" she asked me while chewing on something crunchy. I hesitated before answering.

"No. I didn't."

She sat waiting for me to elaborate.

"I walked home," I said.

Brandy sounded concerned, happy, and proud all in the same breath. It made me happy to hear her response.

"Well, if you can walk home from the gym then you can walk to Zaxby's and grab us a salad," she playfully replied.

"Sure, if you don't mind waiting an hour for your salad!" I jokingly responded. "Now, if this walk and food delivery comes with a reward, I'm sure I can reduce my travel time."

Chapter 45
Re-Vision

As the year came to a close, I had a clearer mind and a better sense of self. December 29, 2015 – the one-year anniversary of the day I lost my sight – would be the day of our first marriage counseling session with the pastor of the church that Brandy attended.

Pastor John Faison, challenged us with exercises, like writing down some of our partner's favorite things and answering questions to see how well we knew one another. He then gave us real-life scenarios dealing with health and finances. He knew about my circumstances, and he gave us some examples of matters couples may face.

"I know you both are thinking, 'We have been through some of this already.' I'm bringing this up because you two have been through a lot together, and you all are moving through it well. You've had your bumps in the road and will continue to, but that's part of the journey. I've had some couples who come in here and can't even decide where they are going to eat on the way home without arguing. You all are still learning, but realize if you can get through all of the things you've been through thus far, then you are already on the right track. Sunny days are easy to endure, but the storms are never far behind. Marriage is a journey in itself and you have to keep working on it, because the next hurdle is coming."

Pastor Faison went on to share some personal things about himself and use his circumstances as learning tools. As the session came to a close, he gave us an assignment to have completed when we returned. We were to think about the reasons we fell in love with one another and what we have grown to love about our partner. Ironically, I had thought about this while in a conversation with my male family members on Christmas. Brandy embodied the idea of a strong woman. She was well put together and strong-spirited, just like my mom. Her ability to be open-minded, assertive, and driven was a good fit to my personable, easy-going, and adventurous personality. After my illnesses, her energy and positive attitude became a counter to my negativity and volatile emotions. She persuaded me to push through my problems and find ways to feel normal. She didn't try to micromanage my circumstances and pull me through them. She didn't try to fix me or my problems. She showed me the understanding and tough love I needed. She loved me through my circumstances while I fixed myself. I wasn't sure what I would get from marriage counseling, but I was happy that we were doing it.

The effort I put toward being positive and regaining my self-confidence started to pay off. I began to re-establish my independence by walking and using ride-sharing services to get out of the house, which did wonders for my attitude and spirit. I reconnected with friends who brought good energy into my life. For example, I began having weekly prayer calls with my friends Reggie McLaurine and Rafael. We gained spiritual growth while we shared our thoughts, experiences and advice with one another.

Reggie and I had come up together playing baseball and football as kids. We stayed close even in high school, but went different ways toward our senior year. There was no love lost. Life just took us in different directions. As adults, we were able to bond over similar experiences we both had on our individual paths, specifically, dealing with grief and the void left from the loss of a loved ones. I lost my mother in high school; he had recently lost his father. We were able to relate to each other because of the trials we had endured. I believed God put us back in each other's lives. In addition to connecting in a way that boosted our spiritual, mental, and emotional health, Reggie and I started going to the gym three days a week in hopes of also improving our physical health.

My asserted efforts toward finding peace gave me an improved outlook on life. Instead of cowering from the world I could no longer enjoy as I did in the past, I faced things head on. I embraced the ways I was learning to function and adapt to my lack of sight. As I learned acceptance, I was able to be more open and engaging with others.

These moments didn't stop with my loved ones. I would find myself in conversations with perfect strangers. It seemed like people would just start talking to me wherever I went. Often, I'd get questions about having two pair of glasses. My health journey would become a topic of conversation and the way people responded showed me how much power could come out of what I had overcome. The story I had was unique and it got people's attention. I had to share what I had dealt with so that others could be inspired, and so I could continue to be encouraged. I felt that God was taking me on a new journey. I just had to accept the challenges that came with it. And I did.

EPILOGUE

On April 30, 2016, Brandy and I gathered with family and friends at the Musicians Hall of Fame and Museum for an intimate wedding ceremony.

Brandy and I would depart for our European honeymoon a few days later, visiting Barcelona, Paris, and Rome. As beautiful as the first two stops were, I enjoyed Rome the most. It was like being thrown in the middle of ancient history. Our visits to the Colosseum and Vatican City left me mesmerized. While I was a little concerned that I wouldn't be able to take in the beauty of Europe, I studied every site we visited, as if I were finding new inspiration.

I left Europe with a much-needed boost. I felt the need to provide more for my family as a husband and father, so I began job searching. After a few weeks, I was offered a job in a local call center. I was grateful for the opportunity, just needing to get my footing in the work environment and start adding value to my household. I knew I would have to adjust with my lack of vision, but I was no longer going to be stifled by my fear of the unknown. I was provided some tools – a larger computer monitor, a screen magnifier, and software – that helps visually impaired individuals. So, it became much easier to work on the computer screen and complete the tasks I was assigned.

As my co-workers would ask questions about my computer screen orientations, I would share some of the happenings of the past few years of my life. No matter who I shared with, they always seemed to get something out of our conversation. Those dark days were in my past, but the impact it was leaving was evident.

About six months after accepting the call center position, I was offered a job with the city government for the Juvenile Justice Center. A few weeks following, I found out that Brandy and I were expecting a daughter. Never before had I been so grateful. I realized the more I pressed forward, the more promising things became. I would have never thought I'd be able to come out a better and stronger person after going through this. I was ready to give up on myself, but I was fortunate to have so much support. I'd find myself in awe at times, especially when I'd look at my chest tattoo in the mirror. It reads "Driving With My Eyes Closed," but what's ironic is that I got that tattoo almost four years before I experienced any of my health issues. I have asked myself, "Was it foresight?" The saying had nothing to do with blindness, but it now fit me like a glove. Life had changed so much and led me far from the course that I had hoped for myself, but it had become a life I was proud of.

I began reviewing more of the videos, voice recordings, and writings I had saved, documenting everything that I had been through: some as stories and others as music and poetry. I continued to make tracks and compose my own songs. I wasn't worried about what would come of this. It was therapy for me. I would have never thought that losing my sight would give me a clearer outlook on my life, but that's how life works. The things we go through are God's way of giving us an opportunity.

Greatness comes from the most uncomfortable of circumstances and sometimes can only be realized by accepting the challenges in front of us. But greatness is not achieved by what you go through; it is achieved by the way you respond and what you're willing to give. It took some time, but I got back in the driver's seat. This time I understood that I couldn't just hit cruise, though. I was going to have to put in more effort than ever before to get back moving how I had always planned. I had found myself stuck in a dark tunnel, lost, but the light was now apparent. The journey wasn't over by a long shot, but I just had to get back on the road and know that everything I had and would experience has a purpose.

www.ingramcontent.com/pod-product-compliance
Lightning Source LLC
Chambersburg PA
CBHW060523130626
46553CB00002B/619